Best of Gravestone Humor

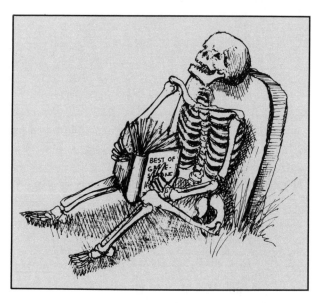

Louis S. Schafer

 Sterling Publishing Co., Inc.   New York

Library of Congress Cataloging-in-Publication Data

Schafer, Louis S.
  Best of gravestone humor / Louis S. Schafer ; illustrated by Elise
Chanowitz.
    p.   cm.
  ISBN 0-8069-7274-2
  1. Epitaphs—Humor.   2. Funeral rites and ceremonies—Humor.
I. Title.
PN6231.E69S3   1990
818'.02—dc20   89-49402
                                                                 CIP

Published by Sterling Publishing Co., Inc.
387 Park Avenue South, New York, N.Y. 10016
Distributed in Canada by Sterling Publishing
% Canadian Manda Group, P.O. Box 920, Station U
Toronto, Ontario, Canada M8Z 5P9
Distributed in Great Britain and Europe by Cassell PLC
Artillery House, Artillery Row, London SW1P 1RT, England
Distributed in Australia by Capricorn Ltd.
P.O. Box 665, Lane Cove, NSW 2066
Manufactured in the United States of America

To Brenda

TABLE OF CONTENTS

INTRODUCTION
BURIAL CUSTOMS

The past two thousand years have brought forth alterations in all phases of life, from medical breakthroughs, political conflicts, and scientific discoveries to industrial revolutions. Yet, perhaps nothing has changed as dramatically as the customs and superstitions surrounding death.

Years ago, as today, living and dying was extremely serious business. Life blended with cessation in a matrimonial bond. People tended to fashion their lifestyles according to what they most desired or deserved after they expired, whether it was everlasting bliss or unimaginable damnation. Therefore, death was envisioned as a mere stepping stone down the road of eternal existence—a condition you created for yourself, depending upon the life you chose to live. Hence, practices involving the dearly departed were of great importance and concern to all.

Funerals, as a result, were events of general interest within each community, and these services were almost always attended by large groups of mourners. Children were allowed, if not encouraged, to participate, in hopes that they might recognize the inevitability of their own mortality. On numerous occasions, in fact, young children were selected to be pallbearers, so that the event would leave an everlasting impression upon them.

Even those who shunned all types of funeral services, such as the early American Puritans, made up for it with a lengthy social gathering at the home of the deceased. Perhaps this was due to the fact that, ordinarily, their social activities were extremely limited.

Most funerals during the 1700s were conducted well after sunset. The quantity and quality of candles stood as a testimonial to the social standing of the deceased. And that was only the beginning.

It was customary for families of the deceased to dole out gifts of thanks to everyone involved in both the arrangements and services. The list of the deserving included family, friends, neighbors, servants, clergy, and attending physicians. It was not uncommon, then, to hand out several hundred dollars worth of crepe, ribbon, scarves, and white linen to those in attendance.

"Mourning jewelry" was collected, cherished, and hoarded. It often carried somber messages of commemoration:

> "Prepared be—follow me,
> Death parts united hearts."

Quite often, mourning jewelry would be fashioned from the hair of the deceased and carefully woven into bracelets, rings, brooches, watch guards, or placed safely within a locket.

Rings made of gold, signifying a "marriage" of body and soul, were also given away. At a single funeral, held in 1738, more than 200 gold mourning rings, valued at $5.00 apiece, were given away. One physician from Salem, Massachusetts, who died in 1758, was discovered to have possessed a large tankard filled with gold rings, which he had gathered over the course of many years of regularly attending funeral services.

Gloves, which were originally thought to keep the spirit of the deceased from entering one's body, were also handed out as a gratuity. In fact, at the services for Andrew Faneuil in Boston, Massachusetts, a record 3,000 pairs of gloves were distributed. And, amazing as it may seem, Dr. Andrew Eliot managed to retain 2,900 pairs of gloves he had collected from individual services during his 32-year stint as pastor of the Old North Church in Boston, Massachusetts. He, and others like him, often earned quite a tidy profit by selling the surplus goods they had hoarded from funerals.

Even people who did not attend a particular service were given one or more of these souvenirs of death. When Judge Sewell refused to take part in the funeral arrangements being conducted for the notoriously evil John Ive, a pair of gloves was still bestowed on him. "I staid at home," he recorded in his diary, "and by that means lost a Ring."

The expense of these services quite often forced families to the very threshold of poverty. A law was passed in the colony of Massachusetts in 1760 forbidding "undue extravagance and display" at funerals. Funeral fervor, however, continued to grow at such an alarming pace that, by the end of the 1700s, long processions of people and horses, all draped proudly in mourning paraphernalia, accompanied the corpse to its final resting place. More than one-fifth of Waitstill Winthrop's entire estate, which amounted to a hefty sum, was spent on his funeral and its appurtenances.

Often, community members who were disliked in life had a difficult time attracting mourners in death. For such occasions, "mourning women" were hired to sit in the front rows of the room, nearest the coffin, and weep for the recently deceased.

The household surroundings and furnishings, as well as the family's attire, were shrouded entirely in black. Tables, chairs, dressers, beds, mirrors and pictures were covered with an ominous dark cloth. Window shutters were tightly secured with a length of black ribbon and were sometimes left that way for months. The family would continue to wear their black mourning clothes for several weeks after the burial, as a true reminder of their deep and unrelenting sorrow. Because the mortality rate of the period was so high, large families sometimes seemed to be wearing black continually.

A "passing bell" was tolled in order to call for prayers from the township's citizens, and also to drive away any "evil spirits" that might have gathered for the funeral. As the corpse lay in state, tradition dictated that the deceased would never be left alone or in total darkness. Candles were lit to fulfill the latter requirement, which also worked to keep evil beings away.

In preparing the corpse for burial, it was an ill omen if the eyes were left open. Hence, in many regions the eyes were held shut by the placement of coins over the lids. Laid in the coffin with its feet pointing east—symbolizing resurrection—the deceased was then removed through the front door and carried to the cemetery.

Superstitious beliefs surrounding funeral processions are still in effect today. Most of us know, for example, the unwritten rule against interrupting the movement of a funeral procession. What we don't remember, however, is the ancient belief that anyone who interrupts the progress of the deceased to the grave will attract the wrath of evil spirits.

The young men who carried the coffin to the gravesite and their more dignified elders, who hoisted the black or purple velvet pall, could expect to return from the services to discover huge quantities of alcohol awaiting them.

The wealthy furnished fine wines, while the poor provided less expensive rum. Even modest funerals could cost the family a goodly sum, as noted on the refreshment list at a funeral for a man who drowned:

"By a pint of liquor for those who dived for him.
. . . By a quart of liquor for those who bro't him home. . . . By two quarts of wine & 1 gallon of

cyder to jury of inquest. . . . By 8 gallons and 3 qts
wine for funeral. . . . By barrel of cyder for
funeral. . . ."

Even paupers, who died destitute and penniless, were buried amid a sea of drink, usually paid for out of the town's
general treasury.

People came from miles away, traversing difficult ter-
rain, to partake in the free handouts of gifts, food, and
alcohol. Intoxication at these events reached such a scan-
dalous point that the town ministers began to preach of its
evils at Sunday services. But the practice was not easily
eradicated.

Burial grounds were sometimes situated quite near the
Meeting House, but some somber services were held as
processions stood in the middle of large plantations. Bur-
ials even took place inside the church, beneath its floor, or
within the walls of the basement. John Adams and his son
John Quincy were both laid to rest inside a church located
in Quincy, Massachusetts. And, old Bruton Parish Church
at Williamsburg is the final resting place for a number of
prominent dignitaries.

Monuments and headstones, which often bore a good
deal of handcrafted symbolism, were constructed of free
rock, slate from nearby quarries, or marble imported from
England. Martha Custis (later Washington) had marble
shipped over from London to place on the grave of her
first husband.

Dozens of generations of mortal men and women lie
buried in this vast cemetery we call the world. They are
laid to rest on hillsides, beneath the shadows of the forests
and in the seas, mouldering under desert sands and fertil-
izing the rolling grasslands of the prairies. A study of these
burial places reveals a great deal about the characteristics
and customs peculiar to the times.

It was customary in decades past for people to prepare
their own inscriptions to be placed upon their tombstones.
If they were not clever at composition, they could hire a

professional "monument poet" or a local preacher to do the job. Most often, however, one gifted family member would be selected to take care of writing a well-phrased epitaph.

In pondering gravestones, we discover a variety of original, quaint, and curious tombstone inscriptions that allow us to look upon a person's life as others did long ago. They speak of religion, love, marriage, occupations, accidents, money, and personal quirks. Often, they are humorous. A 19th-century historian, Alice Morse Earle, aptly described the attitude of many inscription writers: "They seemed to reserve for these gloomy tributes their sole attempt at facetiousness." And, sometimes, the inscriptions are unconsciously humorous—as you will see. . . .

1

CHANCE AND CIRCUMSTANCE

On a given day of any week, you can pick up a newspaper and read about tragic deaths by drowning, fire, traffic accidents, and poisoning, to name just a few. Considering that there are so many potentially lethal hazards surrounding us throughout our lifetimes, the real miracle is that so many of us survive for such a lengthy period.

The most serious challenges to the attainment of "old age," were, of course, wars—declared and undeclared—plagues and other health hazards. Eventually, however, another generation would be born to enjoy the riches left by their forefathers. This new generation, just a few brief years removed, escaped many dangers—but not all!

Scores of people have reached their untimely demise through bursting dams, train derailments, shootings, industrial accidents, and other freak occurrences. Interestingly enough, the people who survived these accidents often wrote haunting memories of tragedy upon their tombstones, rather than recollections of their often long and illustrious lives.

How did they die? Dynamite was a major problem to homesteaders in early America, due to the fact that it was not always stored properly. Often, it would be allowed to freeze during the cold winter season. The nitroglycerine would then settle towards the bottom, where it would become volatile and dangerous to handle. So, from time to time, unexpected explosions were destined to occur.

Gunshot wounds—intentional or unintentional—were often inflicted by farmers, as well as city folk out on their annual hunting excursions. During the late 1800s, it was said that a man who travelled about looking for wild game in thickets and brush would purposely put his shoes on backwards. In this way, if a stray bullet were to fatally injure a trespasser, the shooter could hide in time and avoid being caught. Early settlers, as well as Indians, often used this same trick in pioneer days, and numerous shootings were listed as "accidental."

Cyclones and tornadoes have also been known to cause freakish deaths. A country newspaper article, which was written on a series of twisters that hit the Midwest on May 29, 1879, told of 42 dead and 185 injured. Furthermore, the eyewitness account spoke of horses that had been "swept up in the wind and deposited," frightened and skittish, in strange pastures; of chickens being stripped clean of their feathers; and of extremely fragile personal belongings ending up tens of miles away from home.

In 1896, 30,000 spectators gathered along a lonely stretch of railroad track in Texas to see what had been billed as the most sensational train crash in history. Ironically, William G. Crush, an adventurous executive of the Missouri, Kansas & Texas Railway, was sponsoring the event, which would bring two engines together in a head-on collision at 60 miles per hour. Unfortunately, the show proved to be far more sensational than advertised: a chunk of flying shrapnel maimed two photographers and killed one innocent bystander in the crowd.

Other odd deaths are noted. Eleanor Barry, a 70-year-old woman living alone on Long Island, paid the price for being overly literate. For years, she surrounded herself with every morsel of reading material she could lay her hands on. Books, newspapers, magazines, and department store catalogues were piled from floor to ceiling throughout her modest home. As she lay sleeping one night, one of these huge paper piles teetered and swayed in the darkness, tumbled, and crushed her to death.

Finally, let us not forget Father Cox, of Pittsburgh, who got his name in the history books as the first American priest to hold a Roman Catholic Mass in a dirigible over the Atlantic Ocean. That was the good news for the adventurous priest. The bad news was that he achieved this distinction aboard the ill-fated Hindenburg on May 6, 1937.

Clearly, it can be said that millions of people have left this world beneath a shroud of accidental, mysterious, and sometimes suspicious circumstances. Here is a small sampling of epitaphs dedicated to those who did, indeed, depart ahead of their time.

❦ ❦ ❦

The following was discovered marking the empty grave of a man whose body was lost at sea:
"Under this sod lies John Round
Who was lost at sea and never was found."

❦ ❦ ❦

In memory of a young lady who was killed in one of America's earliest 20th century traffic mishaps:
"The manner of her death was thus
She was druv over by a bus."

Parents may take heed of the following inscription, and watch their young children closely around the house:

"Little Willie from his mirror
Licked the mercury right off,
Thinking, in his childish error,
It would cure the whooping cough.
At the funeral his mother
Smartly said to Mrs. Brown:
'Twas a chilly day for Willie
When the mercury went down.' "

Over the remains of another youngster, killed in a fire:

"Little Willy in the best of sashes,
Played with fire and was burnt to ashes!
Very soon the room got chilly,
But no one liked to poke poor Willy!"

Discovered in a Sussex County graveyard over the remains of two young children:

"Here lie two children
By water confounded,
One died of dropsy
T'other was drownded."

The widow of a man who was blown up in a gunpowder explosion insisted that the following words be placed over his fragmented remains:

"He rests in pieces."

Near Pembrokeshire, Wales:

"Here lie I, and no wonder I'm dead,
For the wheel of the wagon went over my head."

Over the remains of Ann Collins, who obviously lived and drank in King Stanley, the following is inscribed:
"Twas as she tript from cask to cask,
In at a bung-hole quickly fell,
Suffocating was her task,
She had no time to say farewell."

The following commemorative was inscribed in Ross Park Cemetery on the headstone of Henry Harris, who died in 1837, near Williamsport, Pennsylvania:
"Peaceable and quiet, a friend to his father and mother, and respected by all who knew him, and went to the world where horses don't kick. . . ."

On a tombstone found near Huntingdon, the birthplace of Cromwell:
"On the 29th of November
A confounded piece of timber
Came down, bang slam,
And killed I, John Lamb."

From an old Scottish tombstone we learn that we should not trust our friends:"Erected to the memory of
John MacFarlane
Drowned in the Water of Leith
By a few *affectionate* friends."

Found in a small churchyard near Durness:
"Here doth lye the bodie
Of John Flye, who did die
By a stroke from a sky-rocket
Which hit him on the eye-socket."

A piece of wisdom from a youngster who had learned the hard way:

"Fear God,
Keep the Commandments,
and
Don't attempt to climb a tree,
For that's what caused the death of me."

Another tree-climber, Marvin Westbrook, who died in 1824, was buried in Aroostook County, Maine:

"Here I lie
and no wonder I'm dead,
I fell from a tree,
Roll'd over dead."

In memory of one who should have known when it was time to come in out of the weather, even though its "bark" was obviously worse than its "bite":

"Here lies Elizabeth Wise,
Who died of thunder sent from Heaven,
In 1777."

Evidence shows that in the Elmwood Cemetery, situated in Holyoke, Massachusetts, some people are "casually" killed:

"In Memory of
Mr. Nath. Parks
Being out a hunt-
ing and conceal'd
in a Ditch was
Casually shot by
Mr. Luther
Frink."

The following was placed over the joint tomb of three family members run over by a locomotive:

"Listen! Mother, aunt and me
Were killed sudden. Here we be.
We should have no time to missle
Had they blown the engine's whistle."

The words on the following tombstone are contradictory, and it is unclear as to whether the dear departed died during the described incident or not:

"Weep, stranger, for a father spilled
From a stagecoach and *nearly* killed,
His name was John Sykes, a maker of sassengers,
Slain with three other outside passengers."

Over the grave of a man from Belturbet, Ireland:

"Here lies John Higley, whose father and
mother were drowned in their passage
from America; had they both lived
they would have been buried here."

The following humorous slice of history was recorded, almost sarcastically, on a tombstone in Girard, Pennsylvania:

"In memory of
Ellen Shannon
Aged 26 Years
Who was fatally burned
March 21st 1870
by the explosion of a lamp
filled with 'R. E. Danforth's
Non Explosive
Burning Fluid'"

Pumping water out of the well can, indeed, be hazardous to your health:

> "Here lies John Adams, who received a thump
> Right on the forehead from the parish pump,
>   Which gave him the quietus in the end,
>   For many doctors did his case attend."

Inscribed on the tombstone of a man who fell while mountain climbing:

> "Against his will
> Here lies George Hill,
> Who from a cliff
> Fell down quite stiff."

Tucked away in the Old School Baptist Churchyard, located near Roxbury, New York, is a monument listing the strange death of David Corbin:

> "His death was produced by being spured
> in the head by a rooster."

This bit of the past was recorded near Manchester, New York, over the grave of Timothy Ryan in 1814:

> "A thousand ways cut short our days;
>   none are exempt from death.
> A honey bee, by stinging me,
>   did stop my mortal breath."

Evidently, cleanliness is not always healthy, according to Henry Cooke's tombstone, found in Edgartown, Massachusetts:

> ". . . death was caused by bathing. . . ."

Upon the tombstone of young John Rose, who was only ten years old when he decided to go skating one fine winter's day:

> "Dear friends and companions all,
> Pray warning take by me,
> Don't venture on the ice too far
> As 'twas the death of me."

❧ ❧ ❧

In memory of a gentleman who'd gone hunting:

> "A bird, a man, a loaded gun,
> No bird, dead man, Thy will be done."

❧ ❧ ❧

In memory of a young lad who accidentally poisoned himself:

> "Willie had a purple monkey
> Climbing on a yellow stick,
> And when he sucked the paint all off
> It made him deathly sick;
> And in his latest hours he clasped
> The monkey in his hand,
> And bade good-bye to earth
> And went into a better land.
>
> Oh, no more he'll shoot his sister
> With his little wooden gun,
> And no more he'll twist the pussy's tail
> And make her yowl, for fun.
> The pussy's tail now stands out straight;
> The gun is laid aside;
> The monkey doesn't jump around
> Since little Willie died."

2

FAMILY AND FRIENDS

Today's historians often define "Folklore" as the entire body of customs, beliefs, tales, and songs that are handed down, both orally and in writing, from one generation to the next. If we accept this definition, we must conclude that all forms of tombstone inscriptions are an accurate record of family folklore. A vast amount of heritage and memory, in the form of epitaphs, has accumulated through the ages.

When we take the time to consider the "folk" part of folklore, we come to realize a good deal. "Folk," one might assume, certainly may consist of a small group of family members and close friends, residing within a close-knit society all their own. They share with one another their heartfelt opinions and thoughts. What is, in the end, recalled or rejuvenated concerning a particular person's life has no known author or source. It is, by definition, of obscure origin; it could be a family legend or one member's reminiscences. It may cover a wide variety of topics. A special memory might focus on a single conversation or a repulsive habit; it might dwell on an act of heroism or foolishness; or it might reveal a false belief we retain and cherish. This form of folklore is, indeed, the product of true family-type interaction.

Often family members are expected to do a good deal for their relatives. In 1782, when Henry Laurens died, he left the following instructions in his will: "I solemnly enjoin it upon my son as an indispensable duty that, as soon as he conveniently can after my decease, he cause my body to be wrapped in twelve yards of tow cloth, and burnt until it is entirely consumed and then, collecting my ashes, deposit them wherever he may see proper." Dutifully, his son followed the instructions to the letter, giving Laurens the dubious distinction of becoming the first person to be cremated in U.S. history.

During the Civil War, numerous memorable stories evolved concerning the deaths of brave soldiers. In his diary, entitled *Touched With Fire*, Oliver Wendell Holmes tells us of the last words of General John Sedgwick. While commanding the Union forces at Spotsylvania, Sedgwick urged his troops, who had stood by his side for weeks, to charge with: "Come! Come! Why, they couldn't hit an elephant at this dis. . . ."

Throughout history, people have wondered about what specific human characteristic they would be remembered for after they were gone. Family traditions and backgrounds have been told and retold; but personal traits often are lost in the shuffle of the dead, as well as the living. We can learn a great deal from studying epitaphs that touch upon a single aspect of a person's life—whether that aspect be "good" or "bad." And what better group is there to recall such sordid details than family and friends?

Over the remains of a wornout mother from Canterbury:
"Of children in all she bore twenty-four:
Thank the Lord there will be no more."

The following epitaph, found upon a gravestone near Ulster, graphically details just how far caring can go:

"Erected to the Memory of
John Phillips
Accidentally shot
As a mark of affection by his brother."

🦌 🦌 🦌

From the Nettlebed Churchyard, in Oxfordshire:

"Here lies father, and mother, and sister, and I:
We all died within the space of one short year:
They were all buried at Wimble Except I
And I be buried here."

🦌 🦌 🦌

In commemoration of a dedicated missionary, who died in India:

"Here lies the body of the Rev. T. Henry, M.A.,
who long laboured as a Christian missionary
amongst the Rajputs.
He was shot by his chokedar.
'Well done, good and faithful servant.' "

🦌 🦌 🦌

Discovered in St. Andrew's Churchyard, located in Plymouth:

"Here lies the body of James Vernon,
Only *surviving* son of Admiral Vernon."

🦌 🦌 🦌

Like father, like son; or is it the other way around in Grantham:

"John Palfreyman, who is buried here,
Was aged four and twenty year,
And near this place his body lies;
Likewise his father—when he dies."

A unique verse was found marking the grave of Caroline Newcomb, age 4, in Crossroads Cemetery, Vineyard Haven, Massachusetts:
> "She tasted of life's bitter cup,
> Refused to drink the portion up,
> But turned her little head aside,
> Disgusted with the taste and died."

Words written by a disgruntled son living in Maryland:
> "My father and mother were both insane
> I inherited the terrible stain.
> My grandfather, grandmother, aunts and uncles
> Were lunatics all, and yet died of carbuncles."

This is a direct quotation, though we know not exactly where the young gentleman was headed:
> "Gone to meet his mother-in-law!"

Erected by "saddened" relatives:
> "Here lies Peter Montgomery,
> who was accidentally shot in his thirtieth year.
> This monument was erected by grateful relatives."

Found over the grave of a one-month-old baby:
> "Since I am so quickly done for,
> I wonder what I was begun for."

The following headstone recalls that old saying, "What will be, will be":
> "Here lie several of the Stowes,
> Particulars the last day will disclose."

Over the grave of a man who was, evidently, quite content with his situation:

> "Here I lie snug as a bug in a rug."

A relative, who was buried in a nearby grave, was envious enough to have the following etched into his tombstone:

> "Here I lie snugger than that other bugger."

Still another epitaph on the headstone of a youngster:

> "Oped my eyes, took a peep;
> Didn't like it, went to sleep."

It's all that the parents could ask of their seven-year-old daughter, who was buried in Westchester, New York:

> "She done her best."

The parents of this child left no holds barred in order to bring this epitaph into rhyme:

> "Beneath this stone lyes our deare child
> who's gone from we
> For evermore unto eternity;
> Where, us do hope, that we shall go to He,
> But him can ne'er come back again to we."

Discovered near the lighthouse at Holmes Hole, over the remains of three fishermen struck by lightening:

> "Here lie three friends who in their lives
> Were never known to wrangle;
> Holmes Hole
> Cedar Pole
> Cringle, cringle, crangle."

Here is a sad poem written by Robert Crytoft in 1810, at the ripe old age of 90. Apparently, he felt that he had no real friends:

"As I walked by myself I talked to myself,
And thus myself said to me,
Look to thyself and take care of thyself
For nobody cares for thee.
So I turn'd to myself, and I answered myself
In the self-same reverie
Look to myself or look not to myself
The self-same thing will it be."

The following inscription is certainly a unique comparison:

"Mammy and I together lived
Just two years and a half;
She went first—I followed next,
The cow before the calf."

How many people, exactly, are mentioned in this epitaph?:

"1850
In memory of James
and another son
who died in infancy
and five other friends
Erected by James Stewart,
Spirit merchant, Dundee,
and his spouse
and 3 other children."

In Westerville, New York, an epitaph to William Reese speaks of future expectation:

"This is what I expected but *not so soon*."

In the West Woods Graveyard, near Hamden, Connecticut, we find the curious epitaph of five-year-old Milla Gaylord:

<blockquote>
"Soon ripe
Soon rotten
Soon gone
But not forgotten."
</blockquote>

🐦 🐦 🐦

Equally odd is the inscription on the tomb of Sidney Ellis, aged seven weeks, in Center Cemetery, Paxton, Massachusetts:

<blockquote>
"He lived
He wept
He smiled
He groaned
And died."
</blockquote>

🐦 🐦 🐦

Written by a group of mourners whose only wish was that it could have been someone else being laid to rest:

<blockquote>
"Here lies Tom Hyde;
It's a pity that he died;
We had rather
If it had been his father;
If it had been his sister,
We had not missed her;
If the whole generation,
It had been better for the nation."
</blockquote>

🐦 🐦 🐦

The verse found on a headstone in the Calvary Cemetery in Chicago can be read two ways:

<blockquote>
"Cold is my bed, but oh, I love it,
For colder are my friends above it."
</blockquote>

Everyone knew who was responsible for this fine inscription:

"Dear Willie how we miss you,
We miss your pleasant smile,
Your kind little hand.
We never shall see you,
We never shall kiss you,
Till we go to the promised land—
Composed by his mother."

Obviously, the gentleman buried beneath this headstone in Bedwelty did not lead a happy life:

"This poor man wept and the Lord heard him
and delivered him out of all his troubles."

If it hadn't been for one William Stratton, the people still alive would have been fewer:

"Here lies the body of
William Stratton, of Paddington,
buried 18th day of May, 1734, aged 97 years;
who had by his first wife 28 children;
by his second 17, was own father to 45;
grandfather to 86; great-grandfather to 23.
In all 154 children."

This youngster, buried in North Carolina, had an odd name:

"Farewell thou charming little son,
We never shall hear thy voice again
Farewell little E Pluribus Unum
May we together in heaven rich blessings share."

A Shippenburg, Pennsylvania, family used one stone to tell it all:

> "The memory of
> Sam Will Smith
> Who departed this life Nov. 14, 1801.
> This lovely boy near 8 years old,
> Lies Buried with his Brother
> His Sister lies on the one side
> And his Nephew on the other."

And another variation to the same end:

> "Here lies a Father and a Mother true,
> A Granther and a Granny tue."

These grieving parents found something to be cheerful about:

> "Oh! weep for little Johnny, who
> Has gone to his repose,
> His eyes were such a lovely blue,
> His cheeks were like the rose.
> Though his departure grieves us much,
> We must not show contrition,
> For shall we grudge the angels such
> A valuable addition?

We found this curious epitaph over the tomb of David Williams, who died in 1769:

> "Under this Yew tree
> Buried he would be
> Because his father he
> Planted this Yew tree."

The following inscription, from a Birmingham cemetery, tells the living precisely how they compare to the dead—present company excepted, of course.

"O cruel death, so soon to end
Two faithful wives and sincere friends
Death takes the good, too good on earth to stay
And leaves the bad, too bad to take away."

This tombstone, located in Waukegan, Illinois, says it all when it comes to friendship—at least we think it does:

"Words are wanting to say what,
Think what a friend should be,
He was that are."

Certainly, the epitaph of Joanna Farley in Hollis, New Hampshire, exaggerated just a bit:

"Having lived 80 years and having been the
natural parent of *200* offspring, she
died 20th of August 1797."

Over the remains of Ann Jennings, who was remembered for her great ability to give birth:

"Some have children—some have none
Here lies the mother of twenty-one."

3

FOOD AND DRINK

Throughout the years, food and drink, like love and marriage, have gone hand in hand. Humans have partaken in such delectable delicacies as snails, seaweed, chocolate-covered ants, poisonous snakes, and raw fish. As drinkers, we have absorbed into our bloodstreams everything from moonshine to alcohol-tainted mouthwash. And, sadly, on occasions, such actions have been known to cause violent illness and painful death.

Death by ingestion has struck on numerous occasions simply because we have not taken to heart the instructions of Horace Fletcher, who informed us that we should never, under any circumstances, fail to chew each morsel of food at least 32 times (once for each tooth). His philosophy of eating was epitomized in the slogan: "Nature will castigate those who don't masticate." Hundreds of thousands of people throughout the world did, indeed, swallow his dubious theory of digestion. In fact, some mothers diligently told their children to "fletcherize" every bite on their plates.

Perhaps the most well-informed theorist in history concerning health and nutrition was one Dr. G. H. Bigelow.

Formerly employed as the Massachusetts State Health Commissioner, Dr. Bigelow became well known for his intriguing after-dinner speeches. During one such oral presentation, which he offered to a faculty-student group at the Harvard Medical School, he chose for his topic of discussion the hazards of food poisoning. Ironically, more than fifty of his listeners became mysteriously ill from the meal before he had finished his speech.

Health and nutrition have been on the minds of numerous writers through the ages. Two such writers are particularly appropriate to our study. The first, June DeSpain, wrote a hot-selling book in 1977. She was a well-trained writer, but it is the title of her work that we remember: *The Little Cyanide Cook-Book*. The second expert was Dr. Alice Chase, who was best known for writing the book *Nutrition for Health*, which examined eating as a science. Interestingly enough, Dr. Chase died in 1974 of malnutrition.

At the other end of the lengthy spectrum of food consumption we find Frank Reese, who was committed to the idea that he would never die of starvation. As an inmate in the Collin County, Texas, jailhouse, he made it his daily habit to unscrew light-bulbs from their sockets, popping them in his mouth, and chewing them until they could be swallowed. When local newsmen decided to devote a piece to his strange behavior, Reese smiled into the cameras as he consumed no less than fourteen bulbs, as well as the sheriff's sunglasses—with no adverse reaction.

And then there was Glenn Moore, a Californian who loved to drink. As a sales promotion stunt, a West Coast eatery offered customers "all the beer you can drink for a dollar." They were given the opportunity to display their abilities publicly. Moore drank at least two gallons of ale in a period slightly exceeding four hours. Moments later, to the horror of the onlookers, he dropped dead.

Finally, let us not forget Albert Fish, the New York City housepainter, who proved that eating could be quite painful—especially if you are the meal. In 1934, Fish was convicted of murdering and cannibalizing fifteen people. He roasted one of them in a pot of carrots and onions before partaking of his unusual delicacy. For his crimes, Fish was, pardon the expression, "fried."

The moral of the story is that food and drink can certainly cause unexpected death. For a brief period, let us remember those who gave their lives during, or because of, consumption.

❦ ❦ ❦

This memorable epitaph was requested by King Darius:
"Here lies King Darius,
who was able to drink many
bottles of wine
without staggering."

❦ ❦ ❦

In memory of John Randall, who died in 1699:
"Here old John Randall lies
Who counting from his tale
Lived three score years and ten
Such virtue was his Ale.
Ale was his meat,
Ale was his drink
Ale did his heart revive:
And if he could have drunk his Ale
He still would be alive:
But he died
January 5."

❦ ❦ ❦

Or this one:
"My grandfather lies buried here,
My cousin Jane, and two uncles dear;
My father perish'd with inflammation
in the thighs,
And my sister drop't down dead
in the Minories.

But the reason I'm here interr'd, according
to my thinking,
Is owing to my good living and
hard drinking;
If therefore, good Christians, you wish
to live long,
Don't drink too much wine, brandy, gin,
or anything strong."

The error of a stonecutter offers an odd variation on the frequently written epitaph, "My glass is run." On the marker of James Ewins, who was buried in Forest Hill Cemetery, East Derry, New Hampshire, in 1781 is written:
"My glass is Rum."

In the eyes of this writer, the fine art of drinking leads to a long and healthy life:
"She drank good ale, good punch and wine
And lived to the age of 99."

It also seems evident that non-alcoholic beverages can be the cause of your demise:
"Poor Betty Conway
She drank lemonade
At a masquerade
And now she's dead and gone away."

A bit of wit concerning a sermon and a hungry equine:
"The horse bit the parson,
How came that to pass?
The horse heard the parson say,
All flesh is grass."

To Randolph Peter, one of the world's greatest consumers:
"Whoe'er you are, tread softly, I
entreat you,
For if he chance to wake, be sure
he'll eat you."

Eating and etiquette were, from all indications, this man's greatest achievements:
"Here lies one who was born and cried,
Lived three score years and then he died,
His greatest actions that we find,
Were that he washed his hands and dined."

These humorous words, commemorating Joseph Jones, were found near a Wolverhampton church:
"Here lies the bones
of Joseph Jones,
Who ate whilst he was able;
But once o'er fed
He dropt down dead,
And fell beneath the table.

When from the tomb,
To meet his doom,
He rises amidst sinners:
Since he must dwell
In heav'n or hell,
Take him—which gives best dinners."

A bit of unwitting advice found on a Tennessee tombstone:
"She lived a life of virtue and died of the cholera morbus, caused by eating green fruit in hope of a blessed immortality. Reader, go thou and do likewise."

From a New Jersey cemetery, we learn of the hazards to young children who consume too much fruit:
"She was not smart, she was not fair,
But hearts with grief for her are swellin';
All empty stands her little chair:
She died of eatin' water-mellon."

From a New Jersey cemetery, we learn of the hazards to
young children who consume too much fruit:

Poor Anna only slipped up once in life:
"Here lies the body of our Anna
Done to death by a banana
It wasn't the fruit that laid her low
But the skin of the thing that made her go."

Over the remains of a gluttonous man who, evidently, was well known as an habitual overeater:
"Here lies Johnny Cole,
Who died, on my soul,
After eating a plentiful dinner;
While chewing his crust,
He was turned into dust,
With his crimes undigested—poor sinner."

Beware of seafood—so says a Pennsylvania housewife and widow:
"Eliza, sorrowing, rears this marble slab
To her dear John, who died of eating crab."

From a Connecticut tombstone a warning about caffeine:
"Here lies cut down like unripe fruit,
The wife of Deacon Amos Shute:
She died of drinking too much coffee,
Anny Domini—eighteen-foghty."

IT'S ALL IN A NAME

Throughout the ages, legions of "ordinary" people were christened with names that have lived on long after them. Surely, we all have heard of people like Sylvester Graham, the entrepreneur who managed to infuriate Boston bakers by claiming that they had adulterated white bread. "Meat," he further said, "is a powerful constipator which stimulates sexual excess." In retaliation to red meat, Graham went on to invent the whole-wheat wafers that were named in memory of him.

Many other inventive citizens have loaned their names to the items they so ingeniously created. Charles W. Post, for instance, gave us Post Grape Nuts in 1897. William R. Frisbie's Pie Company gave birth to the flying "frisbee" pie tin during the 1870's. And, believe it or not, General Joe Hooker of Civil War fame was responsible for bolstering the morale of his troops, and loaning his name to an entire profession, when he allowed prostitutes to visit his men on the battlefield.

Still, we often forget those whose names seem completely appropriate (or inappropriate) for their habits, occupations, or failings. For example, we should remember one Boston Strawberry of Bonifay, Florida, who was convicted of murder after clubbing an opposing shortstop to death with a bat during a sandlot baseball game. In the end, his life sentence was commuted by Governor Millard Caldwell, who was quoted as saying that "anybody with a name like 'Boston Strawberry' should have a full pardon."

Businessmen have been known, from time to time, to take advantage of a catchy-sounding name. After he earned his first million dollars selling go-carts and snowmobiles, Stanley Fox retired to the warmer climate of Miami, Florida. Soon, however, he grew restless for his home state of Wisconsin, and he returned to trek once again down the long road to fame and fortune. He established Foxy, Incorporated, which caters to people with the same last name as his own. There are fox fur door knockers, fox beer tankards, fox Christmas ornaments, and all types of fox jewelry. Later, Mr. Fox reluctantly admitted that he had, to a point, duped the public: his real name was Fuchs.

And then there is the case of Michael Herbert Dengler of Minnesota, who in 1977 changed his name to "1069." Although the Social Security Administration saw no problem with the change, the local telephone company and the Minnesota Motor Vehicles Department frowned on the request. "One-Zero," as his friends affectionately called him, decided to take his case to court. Sadly, however, although the Minnesota state laws were quite lenient when it came to name changes, One-Zero lost his appeal. Rebellious to the end, he paid his court costs with a check signed "1069."

Certainly last, but perhaps not least, let us give recognition to a lucky gentleman from San Francisco, California, who had the good fortune of being bestowed with the ultimate in names. If you were to list every single living person in the western world in alphabetical order, Zachary Zzzzra would most definitely come at the end.

If nothing else, people do take one thing to the grave

with them, and that is their own name. Hence, let us recall
those who did not become famous for their actions, but
who are remembered in verse because of their somewhat
"punny" titles.

❦ ❦ ❦

The following punning inscription was written for a young
woman named Ann Short:
> "I am short of everything.
> Am Short, o Lord, of praising thee
> Nothing I can do right;
> Needy and naked, poor I be,
> Short, Lord I am of sight!
> How Short I am of love and grace!
> Of everything I'm Short!
> Renew me, then I'll follow place
> Through good and bad report."

❦ ❦ ❦

The following is a musical tribute to take "note" of:
> "On the twenty-second of June,
> Jonathan Fiddle went out of tune."

❦ ❦ ❦

With only one minor change, John Wood's epitaph became
a real tongue twister:
> "Here lies John Bun,
> He was killed by a gun,
> His name was not Bun, but Wood,
> But Wood would not rhyme with gun, but Bun would."

❦ ❦ ❦

Found in a cemetery near Oxford, the following inscription was used for one Mr. Merideth:
> "Here lies one blown out of breath,
> Who lived a merry life, and died a Merideth."

❦ ❦ ❦

Over the tomb of a Mr. Bywater:
>"Here lies the remains of his relative's pride
>Bywater he lived, and Bywater he died;
>Though Bywater he fell, yet Bywater he'll rise
>Bywater baptismal attaining the skies."

The following epitaph is sacred to the memory of Lettuce Manning:
>"Oh, cruel death
>To satisfy thy palate,
>Cut down our Lettuce
>To make a salad."

A peck of everything in life gave Mr. Peck a bushel of respect:
>"Here lies a Peck which some men say
>Was first of all a Peck of clay;
>This, wrought by skill divine while fresh
>Became a curious Peck of flesh.
>Through various forms its Maker ran,
>Then, adding breath, made Peck a man.
>Full fifty years Peck felt life's bubbles,
>Till death relieved a Peck of troubles.
>Then fell poor Peck, as all things must,
>And here he lies, a Peck of dust."

The following name, from a Skaneateles, New York, cemetery, was changed—not to protect the innocent, but to make it into correct verse:
>"Underneath this pile of stones
>Lies all that's left of Sally Jones.
>Her name was Lord, it was not Jones,
>But Jones was used to rhyme with stones."

The widow of this man was forced to change only a portion of his name:

"Here lie the remains of Thomas Woodhen,
The most amiable of husbands and excellent of men.
His real name was woodcock, but it
Wouldn't come in rhyme.—His widow."

Found in the Peterborough Cathedral cemetery, over the grave of Richard Worme:

"Does worm eat Worme?
Knight Worme this truth confirms:
For here, with worms, lies Worme,
a dish for worms.

Does Worme eat worm?
Sure Worme will this deny,
For worms with Worme,
a dish for Worme don't lie.

'Tis so, and 'tis not so,
for free from worms
'Tis certain Worme is
blessed without his worms."

A true bit of knowledge can sometimes be found in a name:

"To the memory of Susan Mum
Silence is wisdom."

In commemoration of Henry Best, who left this world in 1629:

"My time is short, the longer is my rest
God calls them soonest whom he loves the Best."

Over the grave of a gentleman whose name simply wouldn't do:

"Underneath this ancient pew
Lie the remains of Jonathan Blue;
His name was Black, but that wouldn't do."

This man, evidently, died to save his fellow citizens:

"Here lies a Foote
Whose death may thousands save;
For Death now has one foot
Within the grave."

Never on Sunday, yet perhaps on Munday ("pelf" means money or riches):

"Hallowed be the Sabaoth,
And farewell all worldly Pelfe;
The Week begins on Tuesday,
For Munday hath hang'd himself."

On the gravestone of Robert Miles, who went that-a-way:

"This tombstone is a Milestone;
Hah! how so?
Because beneath lies Miles who's
Miles below."

The following was inscribed to commemorate the Vicar Chest, of Chepstow Church:

"Here lies at rest, I do protest,
One Chest within another,
The chest of wood was very good;
Who says so of the other?"

On the grave of Thomas All, who had it all:
>"Reader, beneath this marble lies
>All that was noble, good, and wise;
>All that once was formed on earth,
>All that was of mortal birth;
>All that liv'd above the ground,
>May within this grave be found:
>If you have lost or great or small,
>Come here and weep, for here lies All;
>Then smile at death, enjoy your mirth,
>Since God has took his All from earth."

The following inscription was discovered in an Old English churchyard near Pembroke:
>"Here under this sod and under these trees
>Is buried the body of Solomon Pease.
>But here in his hole lies only his pod
>His soul is shelled out and gone up to God."

Over the remains of one Theophilus Cave, who died in 1584, we find an interesting play on words:
>"Here in this grave there lies one Cave:
>We call a Cave a grave.
>If Cave be grave, and grave be Cave
>Then reader judge I crave
>Whether both Cave be in this grave
>Or grave lie here on Cave:
>If grave in Cave here would lie
>Then grave, where is thy victory?
>
>Go reader and report
>Here lies a Cave
>Who conquers death
>And buries his own grave."

In memory of one Mr. Day, who was remembered for his height:

> "As long as long can be,
> So long so long was he;
> How long, how long, dost say?
> As long as the longest Day."

Let us remember the music conductor, who went by the name of Stephen:

> "Stephen and Time are now both even;
> Stephen beat Time, and now Time's beat Stephen."

This memorable epitaph was found over the remains of Thomas Partridge, whose untimely death was in the month of May:

> "What! Kill a partridge
> In the month of May,
> Not quite sportsman-like
> Eh, Death, eh?"

The following epitaph was found on the headstone of Eliza More:

> "Here lies one who never lied before,
> And one who never will lie More,
> To which there need be no More said."

Written by the wife of Thomas More:

> "More had I once, More would I have,
> More is not to be had:
> The first I lost, the next is vain
> The third is too too bad.
> If I had used More with more regard,
> The More that I did give,

I might have made More use and fruit
Of More while he did live.
But time will be recalled no More,
More since is gone in brief.
Too late repentance yields no More
Save only pain and grief.
My comfort is that God hath More
Such Mores to send at will,
In hope whereof I sigh no More
But rest upon him still."

A punning memory given to the Earl of Kildare:
"Who killed Kildare?
Who dare Kildare to kill?
Death killed Kildare,
Who dare kill whom he will."

After Elizabeth White was married to Humphrey Brown, there was an opportunity for the following inscription over their graves:
"Here lies a Brown and White, the colors one,
Pale, drawn by death, here shaded by a stone:
One house did hold them both whilst life did last,
One grave do hold them, now life is past."

In memory of a Mr. Fish, whose name was used as an interesting twist of fate:
"Worms are bait for fish
But here's a sudden change,
Fish is bait for worms—
Is not that passing strange?"

The following inscription is a curious remembrance of
Roger Earth:
> "From Earth we came, to Earth we must return
> Witness this Earth that lies within this Urn.
> Begot by Earth; born also of Earth's womb,
> 74 years lived Earth, now Earth's his tomb
> In earth Earth's body lies under this stone
> But from this earth to Heaven Earth's soul is gone."

Both in life and death, this gentleman's name was Mudd:
> "Here lies Matthew Mudd,
> Death did him no hurt;
> When alive he was Mudd,
> But now he's only dirt."

One might ask, was there a sex-change for this old woman?
> "Here lies Ann Mann.
> She lived an old maid
> But died an old Mann."

---------------- 5 ----------------

LOVE AND MARRIAGE

Marriage, in one form or another, has been around since the beginning of civilization, and people have "tied the knot," as the saying goes, for a variety of reasons. Unhappy marriages, however, seem to attract the most attention, often ending up in front of a courtroom judge, with grounds running the spectrum from incompatibility to mental cruelty.

Take the case of Solomon Fegion, a resident of Stockton, California. At the ripe old age of 103, he was sued by his 100-year-old wife on grounds that he had committed adultery. The judge ruled in favor of Mrs. Fegion, despite the argument by her husband that "a woman looks like a man to me now."

In another court case—this one in 1656—a Captain Kemble, of Boston, Massachusetts, was found guilty of "lewd and unseemly behavior." The punishment was that he be placed in stocks for no less than two hours. Captain Kemble's outrageously "vulgar," almost unforgivable, behavior was to kiss his wife in public on the Sabbath after a three-year sojourn at sea.

Often, instead of love *or* money being the reason for marriage, it's the love *of* money that does the trick. And such a foundation for a relationship can lead to unforgettable criminal behavior.

"Women are all right in their place," Johann Hoch told reporters, "but marry only one." Certainly, this dapper little, nearsighted German-American knew what he was talking about. Over a period of 18 years, Hoch managed to tie the knot with between forty-five and fifty women of various backgrounds, ages, and descriptions. The reason for most of his marriages was to cheat his wives out of their life savings or inheritance. And when that wasn't the reason—in more than a dozen cases—he murdered his wives for their insurance money, poisoning them with lethal doses of arsenic.

Taken into custody by New York City police officers, Hoch confessed to his murderous ways. And, as a legacy, he revealed six tried-and-true methods of winning a lady's heart, claiming (1) 90 percent of all women can be won by flattery, (2) a man should never let a woman know her faults, (3) a man should always appear to a woman to be the anxious one, (4) the average man can fool the average woman if he will let her have her own way, (5) women like to be told complimentary things about themselves, and (6) when a man makes love, he should be ardent and earnest. What he said might well have been true, but in the end, Hoch was extradited to Chicago, and hanged in 1905.

This sampling of epitaphs concerning love and marriage is not as deadly, but most of their authors seem to believe that marriage is far worse than other types of "institutions."

Over the remains of a tired wife and mother, in Pembroke, Massachusetts:

"Here lies a poor woman who always was tired,
She lived in a house where help wasn't hired.
The last words she said were 'Dear friends, I am going,
Where washing ain't wanted, nor mending, nor sewing.
There all things is done exact to my wishes,

For where folks don't eat there's no washing of dishes.
In heaven loud anthems forever are ringing,
But having no voice, I'll keep clear of singing
Don't mourn for me now, don't mourn for me never;
I'm going to do nothing forever and ever.' "

The headstone of this wife from Devonshire recalls how she broke that wedding vow, "Love, Honor, and Obey":
"Charity, wife of Gideon Bligh,
Underneath this stone doth lie.
Nought was she e'er known to do
That her husband told her to."

Evidently, the husband of Jennie E. Wilson, who was buried in College Hill Cemetery, Lebanon, Illinois, was surprised to have been so lucky in love:
"She was more to me than I expected."

From this Essex, England, epitaph, it is quite clear who was the boss in this family:
"Here lies the man Richard,
And Mary his wife,
Whose surname was Prichard:
They lived without strife:
And the reason was plain,—
They abounded in riches,
They had no care nor pain,
And his wife wore the britches."

There was a reason that this Welsh farmer loved flowers:
"This spot is the sweetest I've seen in my life,
For it raises my flowers and covers my wife."

Over the remains of a wife's tomb:
"Husband, prepare to follow me!"

❦ ❦ ❦

Later, the following inscription was added by her husband:
"I cannot come, my dearest life,
For I have married another wife.
And much as I would come to thee,
I now must live and die with she."

❦ ❦ ❦

A widower placed the following intermittent message over
his wife's tomb:
"1890. The light of my Life has gone out.
1891. I have struck another match."

❦ ❦ ❦

What twelve dollars could buy in Burlington, Massachu-
setts:
"Sacred to the memory of Anthony Drake,
Who died for peace and quietness sake;
His wife was constantly scolding and scoffin',
So he sought for repose in a twelve-dollar coffin."

❦ ❦ ❦

On the tomb of one who was remembered for her re-
straint:
"She was married twenty-six years and in all that time
never once banged the door."

❦ ❦ ❦

Over the remains of a wife, who hoped to keep a secret:
"Resurgam—(I am risen.)"
Further down, she had this to add:
"But don't tell my husband of it."

❦ ❦ ❦

John Dryden composed the following epitaph for his wife:
"Here lies my wife: here let her lie!
Now she's at rest, and so am I."

This gentleman, from Arlington, Virginia, was happily un-married for seven, wonderful years:
"Here lies the body of John Custis, who died, aged 77
years; and yet lived but 7, being the time of his
keeping a bachelor's house at Arlington, on the
eastern shore of Virginia."

An unusual log-shaped marker to Emily Spear, in Glen-dale Cemetery, Cardington, Ohio, offers this quaint epi-taph:
"My husband
promised me
that my
body should
be cremated
but other
influences
prevailed."

Over the grave of a man who was said to have "beaten" two of his most cherished possessions:
"Here lies John Dove who varied his life
As a beater of gold by beating his wife."

A happy, tearful gentleman placed the following over his wife in New Hampshire:
"Tears cannot restore her—therefore I weep."

This henpecked husband was happy when his wife died:
> "Here lies my wife in earthly mould,
> Who when she lived did naught but scold.
> Peace! wake her not, for now she's still,
> She had; but now I have my will."

❦ ❦ ❦

We suspect that David Goodman Croly's epitaph, in Evergreen Cemetery, Lakewood, New Jersey, was composed by his wife:
> "He meant well,
> Tried a little,
> Failed much."

❦ ❦ ❦

At least this woman from Burlington, Vermont, had something to look forward to:
> "She lived with her husband fifty years
> And died in the confident hope of a better life."

❦ ❦ ❦

In Potterne, Wilts, one epitaph recalls the best of two evils:
> "Here lies Mary, the wife of John Ford,
> We hope her soul is gone to the Lord;
> But if for Hell she has chang'd this life
> She had better be there than be John Ford's wife."

❦ ❦ ❦

Near Burlington, Vermont, we find this interesting tombstone inscription:
> "Here lies the wife of Brother Thomas,
> Whom tyrant death has torn from us,
> Her husband never shed a tear,
> Until his wife was buried here.
> And then he made a fearful rout,
> For fear she might find her way out."

❦ ❦ ❦

A simple warning to the unwary:
    "Here lies, thank God, a woman who
Quarrelled and stormed her whole life through;
    Tread softly o'er her mouldering form,
    Or else you'll rouse another storm."

The following inscription was found in a country church-yard:
    "Here lies the body of James Robinson, and
            Ruth his wife.
    Their warfare is accomplished."

In memory of a man who never was married:
    "At threescore winters' end I died,
    A cheerless being, sole and sad,
    The nuptial knot I never tied—
    And wish my father never had."

The following tombstone was unearthed near Radnorshire, England:
    "I plant these shrubs upon your grave, dear wife,
    That something on this spot may boast of life.
    Shrubs must wither and all earth must rot;
Shrubs may revive: but you, thank heaven, will not."

In memory of Anna Lovett:
    "Beneath this stone and not above it
    Lie the remains of Anna Lovett;
    Be pleased, dear reader, not to shove it,
    Lest she should come again above it.
    For 'twixt you and I, no one does covet
    To see again this Anna Lovett."

In memory of Joan Carthew, buried in a St. Agnes church-yard, who explained that it was often quite easy to make certain decisions:

> "Here lies the body of Joan Carthew,
> Born at St. Columb, died at St. Cue;
> Children she had five,
> Three are dead, and two alive;
> Those that are dead choosing rather
> To die with their mother than live with their father."

Over the remains of James Danner of Louisville, who was laid to rest with four of his former wives:

> "An excellent husband was this Mr. Danner,
> He lived in a thoroughly honorable manner,
> He may have had troubles,
> But they burst like bubbles,
> He's at peace now, with Mary, Jane, Susan
> and Hannah."

Apparently, this fellow had a lot to be grateful for:

> "Here lies my poor wife
> Without bed or blanket,
> But dead as a door nail,
> And God be thankit."

The following inscription was placed on the tombstone of a Quaker gent's second wife:

> "Here lies wife second of old Wing Rogers,
> She's safe from cares and I from bothers;
> If death had known thee as well as I,
> He ne'er had stopped, but passed thee by,
> I wish him joy, but much I fear,
> He'll rue the day he came thee near."

From a cemetery near Sheffield, England:
> "Stay, bachelor, if you have wit,
> A wonder to behold!
> A husband and wife in one dark pit,
> Lie close and never scold!
> Tread softly, though, for fear she wakes—
> Hark! she begins already!
> 'You've hurt my head—my shoulder aches;
> These sots can ne'er move steady,'
> Ah, Friend, with happy freedom blest!
> See how my hope's miscarried!
> Not death itself can give you rest,
> Unless you die unmarried."

In Hollis, New Hampshire, both husband and wife had something to be thankful for:
> "Here lies Cynthia, Stevens' wife
> She lived six years in calms and strife.
> Death came at last and set her free,
> I was glad and so was she."

The following epitaph was composed by a fearful husband:
> "Within this grave do lie,
> Back to back my wife and I.
> When the last trump the air shall fill,
> If she gets up I'll just lie still."

This epitaph concerns an overdue wedding day:
> "The wedding day appointed was
> And wedding clothes provided,
> But ere that day did come, alas!
> He sickened and he die did."

Over the remains of a woman who was married to the Parish Clerk:

> "The children of Israel wanted bread,
> And the Lord he sent them manna,
> Old clerk Wallace wanted a wife,
> And the Devil he sent him Anna."

One husband wrote the following inscription on his wife's tombstone, in memory of her and her neighbors:

> "Here is my much loved Celia laid,
> At rest from all her earthly labours!
> Glory to God! Peace to the dead!
> And the ears of all her neighbors."

In negativity, this couple was very agreeable:

> "Here lies John and with him Mary,
> Cheek by jowl, and never vary;
> No wonder that they so agree,
> John wants no punch, and Mary no tea."

The following was written by a man who wanted to "kill two birds with one (head) stone":

> "Here lies the body of Sarah Sexton,
> She was a wife that never vexed one.
> I can't say as much for her on the next stone."

Happiness must equal some other type of addition:

> "Here lies a noble pair, who were in name,
> In heart, in mind, and sentiment the same,
> The Arithmetic Rule then can't be true,
> For one and one did never here make two."

This wife's "grieving" mood could last indefinitely:
"Sacred to the memory of Jared Bates,
Who died August the 6th, 1800:
His widow, age 24, lives at 7 Elm Street,
Has every qualification for a good wife,
And yearns to be comforted."

Over the grave of a poet, who was happy to escape:
"Here let a bard unenvied rest
Who no dull critic dare molest,
Escaped from the familiar ills
Of thread-bare coat and unpaid bills;
From rough bum-bailiff's upstart duns,
From sneering pride's detested sons,
From all those pest'ring ills of life,
From, worst of all, a scolding wife."

The following epitaph was found over the remains of a
married couple:
"A.D. 1827: I am anxiously expecting you."

Forty years later, these words were added:
"A.D. 1867: Here I am."

Found in a small cemetery near Montrose:
"Here lies the bodeys of George Young and Isabel
Guthrie, and all their posterity for fifty years
backwards."

In memory of a gent who wasn't always faithful to his wife, and those who buried him knew it:

"Erected to the memory of Alexander Gray,
some time farmer in Mill of Burns, who died
in the 96th year of his age, having had 32
legitimate children by two wives."

❦ ❦ ❦

This poetic epitaph was discovered in Norfolk, Connecticut:

"Lieut. Nathan Davis.
Died in 1781.
Death is a debt that's justly due,
That I have paid and so must you."

❦ ❦ ❦

Side by side with that headstone, another curious epitaph was written:

"Elizabeth, wife of Nathan Davis.
Died in 1786.
This debt I owe is justly due,
And I am come to sleep with you."

❦ ❦ ❦

In the Woodland Cemetery, in Philadelphia, Pennsylvania, two headstones stand side-by-side, which read:
"Father"   "Mother"

Joining the two is a single arch bearing the following:
"Divided in life—United in death."

❦ ❦ ❦

6

OCCUPATIONS

Occupational hazards have been a part of both life and death since man first used a stick to plow the earth. For their life's calling, people the world over have risked everything in their line of work, from finances to friendship, to their very own lives. Too, they sometimes used their occupational expertise in heinous crimes against their fellow men. In numerous cases they succeeded; but often the risks were too large or their expertise too little.

Take the case of Dr. Arthur Waite who, in 1916, attempted to make use of his years of medical experience in the job of poisoning his father-in-law, John Peck. Initially, Waite administered a lethal dose of diphtheria toxin into Mr. Peck's dinner, but the old man wasn't phased. Next, the unscrupulous physician used a nasal spray spiked with deadly tuberculosis germs. This, too, failed to get the desired result. Time and again, Waite continued to devise new approaches to the problem, trying a draught of calomel, then typhoid bacteria, and next influenza. Each time, however, John Peck survived. Finally, dispensing with this odd germ warfare, the frenzied doctor murdered the old codger with a hefty dose of arsenic. Poison, however, was obvious to the authorities, and Dr. Waite was captured and sentenced to spend the remainder of his life in prison.

With the cost of real estate going up and up, even in cemeteries, perhaps we should take heed of inventor Philip Bachman. This ingenious mortician has devised a somewhat remarkable, if not morbid, process by which we can save thousands of dollars on the cost of burial plots. To put it briefly, his patented idea proposes to freeze the remains of the dear departed in liquid nitrogen at approximately 150 degrees below zero, and then to run them through a "surface enhancing" machine. In reality, this gruesome contraption pulverizes the corpse into hundreds of smaller pieces, like freeze-dried coffee crystals. Finally, the re-collected chunks of our loved ones would be deposited into small funeral urns. Fortunately, no one really understands what might happen if boiling water were inadvertently poured over the remains.

"All the news that is the news" might have been the catchphrase of Chris Chubbuck, a newscaster from Sarasota, Florida. One day in 1974, Chris guaranteed that she herself would be on the evening news. She concluded a broadcast by strongly denouncing station policies, and then, without hesitation, drew out a handgun and shot herself in the head.

Finally, let us not forget the "fortunate" misfortune of David Kennison, politician. In the Battle of Sackett's Harbor, during the War of 1812, Kennison's hand was blown off, yet he survived. Some years later, the limb of a tree fell on his head and fractured his skull, yet he survived. Then, while he was a member of the Massachusetts State Militia, both of his legs were severely splintered by a misfired cannon; yet he survived. Though the fractures healed, Kennison was forever plagued with festering sores. Still later, a horse happened to kick him violently in the face, causing permanent disfigurement—yet, the healthy old politician lived on. Eventually, Kennison would expire in 1851, at the ripe old age of 115. He has gone down in history as the longest-surviving person who took part in the Boston Tea Party.

Occupational accidents happen every day, and some folks live to tell about them. Here are a few, however, who didn't fare as well.

❦ ❦ ❦

In memory of Mrs. Oldfield, an actress:
> "This we must own in justice to her shade
> 'Tis the first bad exit Oldfield ever made."

❦ ❦ ❦

This well-respected astronomer probably doesn't get much respect today in Elmwood Cemetery, East Otisfield, Maine:
> "Prof. Holden the
> old astronomer
> discovered that the
> Earth is flat and
> Stationary, and that
> the sun and moon do move."

❦ ❦ ❦

Let us not forget the "kneads" of a baker:
> "Throughout his life he kneaded bread
> And deemed it quite a bore.
> But now six feet beneath earth's crust
> He needeth bread no more."

❦ ❦ ❦

There once lived a humorous physician, rejoicing in the name of I. Letsome, who proposed his own epitaph:
> "When people's ills, they come to I
> I physics, bleeds, and sweats 'em;
> Sometimes they live, sometimes they die;
> What's that to I? I. Letsome."

Over the grave of a gentleman who built houses for a living:

> "Under this stone, reader, survey
> Dead Sir John Vanbrugh's house of clay.
> Lie heavy on him, earth! for he
> Laid many heavy loads on thee."

Discovered in Gateshead, Durham, over the remains of another architect:

> "Here lies Robert Trollope,
> Who made yon stones roll up;
> When death took his soul up,
> His body filled this hole up."

In memory of Ephraim Wales Bull, laid to rest in Sleepy Hollow Cemetery, Concord, Massachusetts. He was a successful farmer, but a terrible business man:

> "He sowed, others reaped."

A monument shaped like a drummer's sample case reminds us that Thomas W. Campbell, buried in Aspen Grove Cemetery, Burlington, Iowa, was a travelling salesman:

> "My Trip is Ended.
> Send My Samples Home."

A one-time high school teacher and principal, S. B. McCracken, wrote his own epitaph in an Elkhart, Indiana, cemetery:

> "School is out
> Teacher has gone home"

Fitting words in memory of an author:
> "Here lies an author—pray forgive
> The work that fed his pride;
> Long after death he thought to live,
> And long before it died."

In the memory of a not-so-honest newspaper editor:
> "Here 'lies' an Editor!
> 'Snooks,' if you will;
> In mercy, Kind Providence,
> Let him 'lie' still!
> He 'lied' for his living: so
> He lived while he 'lied':
> When he could not 'lie' longer
> He lied down and died."

Lorenzo Ferguson, a journalist, was buried in Crown Hill Cemetery, Atlanta, Georgia, where his stone is identified by his pen name and a humorous comment:
> "Fuzzy
> Woodruff
> 1884–1929
> 'Copy All In' "

In memory of one Edward Pardon, who spent his life selling books:
> "Here lies poor Ned Pardon, from misery freed,
> Who long was a bookseller's hack;
> He led such a damnable life in this world,
> I don't think he'll ever come back."

The following can be found over the grave of the town coroner, who hanged himself:

"He lived and died
By suicide."

Here's what a gravedigger thought about wealth:

"Here lie I at the chapel door,
Here lie I because I'm poor,
The farther in the more you'll pay,
Here lie I as warm as they."

On the tombstone of a dentist:

"View this gravestone with gravity
He is filling his last cavity."

Over the grave of a fisherman from Block Island, Rhode Island:

"He's done a catching cod
And gone to meet his God."

Above an avid fisherman, who made his living near Ripon, York:

"Here lies poor but honest
Bryan Tunstall
He was a most expert angler
until Death, envious of his art
threw out his line, hooked him
and
landed him here the 21st day of April
1790."

A log-shaped gravestone in Island Cemetery, Newport, Rhode Island, is dedicated to a carpenter named Isaac Thurston:

"He sawed logs for forty years
But he won't saw this one."

🐛 🐛 🐛

The entire town commemorated one of its mayors, which would appear to have been a rather gleeful affair:

"Here lies John, late Mayor of Dundee
Here lies Him, here lies He,
A. B. C. E. F. G.
Di Do Dum, Di Do Dee."

🐛 🐛 🐛

A congregation recalled its organ player in Bluntsham, 1621:

"Under this stone lies Meredith Morgan
Who blew the bellows of our Church Organ;
Tobacco he hated, to smoke most unwilling,
Yet never so pleased as when pipes he was filling;
No reflection on him for rude speech could be cast,
Tho' he gave our old organ many a blast."

🐛 🐛 🐛

Over the grave of a man who held the dubious occupation of being a pig-slaughterer:

"Here lies John Higgs,
A famous man for killing pigs,
For killing pigs was his delight,
Both morning, afternoon, and night,
Both heats and colds he did endure,
Which no physician could e'er cure.
His knife is laid, his work is done;
I hope to heaven his soul is gone."

Over the grave of a fine cook, who was celebrated for his culinary creations:
> "Peas to his hashes.
> (Peace to his ashes.)"

Please remember the auctioneer:
> "Beneath this stone, facetious wight,
> Lies all that's left of poor Joe Wright.
> Few heads with knowledge more informed,
> Few hearts with friendship better warmed.
> With ready wit and humour broad
> He pleased the peasant, squire, and lord;
> Until grim death, with visage queer,
> Assumed Joe's trade of Auctioneer;
> Made him the Lot to practice on,
> With 'going, going,' and anon
> He knocked him down to 'Poor Joe's gone!' "

The following inscription was found over the remains of Abraham Newland, a banker from London, England:
> "Beneath this stone old Abr'am lies:
> Nobody laughs and nobody cries:
> Where he's gone or how he fares,
> No one knows and no one cares."

Over the remains of gentleman who was given the shameful distinction of being the one responsible for inventing spectacles:
> "Here lies Salvino Armalo D'Armati,
> of Florence,
> the inventor of spectacles.
> May God pardon his sins!
> The year 1318."

Words to remember a man who just couldn't seem to find
the right job:

> "Here lies John Bairf in the only place for which he
> never applied."

In memory of Sir John Strange, an attorney:

> "Here lies an honest lawyer—
> This is Strange."

On the headstone of a landlord:

> "Here lies the Landlord of 'The Lion,'
> His hopes removed to lands of Sion,
> His wife, resigned to Heaven's will,
> Will carry on the business still."

Just two years later, the landlord's wife was interred beneath this quaint inscription:

> "Here lies the Landlord's loving wife,
> Her soul removed from lands of strife.
> She's gone aloft her spouse to tell
> The Inn he left her turned out well."

The following words were placed over the grave of a bar-
tender, uttered in death, but never in life:

> "This is on me, boys!"

In St. Michael's Churchyard, located in Aberystwyth, the
following inscription was etched in memory of a young
hosier who had a sweetheart named Hannah:

> "He left his hose, his Hannah, and his love
> To sing Hosannahs in the world above."

To the very end, this young lady was a Maid of Honor:
> "Here lies (the Lord have mercy on her)
> One of her Majesty's maids of honour:
> She was young, slender, and pretty;
> She died a maid—the more's the pity."

The following was written in commemoration for P. T. Barnum's fat lady of the circus:
> "Grease, but living grease no more!"

Over the remains of a famous clown named Grimaldi:
> "Here I am!"

In memory of a song writer:
> "He has gone to the only place where
> His own works are excelled."

Boy, could she perform well in the kitchen:
> "Beneath this dust
> Lies the smouldering crust
> Of Eleanor Batchelor Shoven,
> Well versed in the arts
> of pies, puddings, and tarts
> And the lucrative trade of the oven.
>
> When she'd lived long enough
> She made her last puff,
> A puff by her husband much praised,
> And now she doth lie
> and makes a dirt pie
> And hopes that her crust will be raised."

Over the grave of Lord Brougham, who was a learned
orator:
> "Here, reader, turn your weeping eyes,
>   My fate a useful moral teaches;
>   The hole in which my body lies
> Would not contain one half my speeches."

In a quiet, little churchyard in South Wales we find this
inscription to the parish parson:
> "Hurrah! my boys, at the Parson's fall,
>   For if he'd lived he'd a'buried us all."

It seems that this 19th century parish clerk was a man of
many trades:
> "Silent in dust lies mould'ring here
>   A Parish Clerk of voice most clear;
>   None Joseph Rogers could excel
>   In laying bricks or singing well."

The following punning epitaph is found over the grave of
an Irish grocer:
> "Here lie the remains of John Hall, grocer,
>   The world is not worth a *fig*, and I have
>   good *raisins* for saying so."

In the end, poor Frank was forced to exchange places with
another:
> "Here lies the body of poor Frank Row,
>   Parish Clerk, and grave stone cutter.
>   And this is writ to let you know,
>   What Frank for others used to do,
>   Is now for Frank done by another."

This Cardinal was, evidently, good at some things in life:
"Here lies a Cardinal who wrought
Both good and evil in his time.
The good he did was good for naught
Not so the evil—it was prime."

According to this locksmith, there's more than one way to get into heaven:
"A zealous locksmith died of late,
And did arrive at heaven's gate;
He stood without and would not knock,
Because he meant to pick the lock."

This politician won the most important election of his life:
"For eternal salvation
He received nomination,
And as he expected,
Was duly elected."

Apparently, this doctor, buried in Pine Log Cemetery, Brookland, Arkansas, hoped to continue his practice in the next world:
"Dr. Fred Roberts
1875–1931
Office Upstairs."

No treatment in the world could have saved this doctor:
"Here lies the body of Dr. Bowen
Caught when death was out a mowin',
Used to curing others' ills—
Yet his homeopathic pills,
Couldn't keep the Doc from goin'."

Over the remains of an over-active midwife:
"In memory of
Mrs. Phebe Crewe
Who died May 28, 1817,
Aged 77 years.
Who during forty years
practice as a midwife
in this city, brought into
the world nine thousand,
seven hundred and
thirty children."

❦ ❦ ❦

In memory of a lonely housekeeper:
"Be not afraid to venture near this stone!
Of naught contagious did she die,
The maid who rests beneath this stone
She died of 'constancy' alone."

❦ ❦ ❦

Poor and destitute, Simon felt he made the right choice:
"Shed a tear for Simon Ruggle,
For life to him was a constant struggle,
He preferred the tomb and death's dark state,
To managing mortgaged real estate."

❦ ❦ ❦

The following epitaph was composed by a marble cutter,
who believed in advertising his wares—no matter what:
"Here lies Jane Smith,
Wife of Thomas Smith, Marble Cutter
This monument was erected by her
husband as a tribute to her memory
and a specimen of his work.
Monuments of this same style are
two hundred and fifty dollars."

❦ ❦ ❦

In memory of a confused warehouse worker:
"Samuel Gardner was blind in one eye and in a
moment of confusion he stepped out of a receiving and
discharging door in one of the warehouses into the ineffable glories of the celestial sphere."

And let us remember a woodcutter from Ockham, Surrey:
"The Lord saw good, I was lopping off wood,
And down fell from the tree:
I met with a check, and broke my neck
And so death lopped off me."

In the memory of John Bilbie, who made a career out of
repairing watches:
"Bilbie, thy
Movements kept in play
For thirty years and more we say,
Thy balance or thy
Mainspring's broke
And all thy movements cease to work."

7

THE ROOT OF ALL EVIL

Even before mankind began to record historical events, the driving force behind the vast majority of societies throughout the world was the need and desire to secure money—or its equivalent—and hold onto it. People have been known to steal, cheat, swindle, counterfeit, invest, gamble, play, and even work for a living. Obviously, at times, our total existence here on earth has been controlled by that all-encompassing urge to get rich quick and stay rich until we die.

Men and women throughout the ages have gone to extraordinary lengths to gain access to vast amounts of wealth. Sometimes they are bizarre. Take the case of George Dashnau, a Philadelphia, Pennsylvania, advertising agent, who was head and shoulders above the rest when it came to money-making schemes.

In the mid-1970's, Dashnau opened the first-of-its-kind mail-order supply house specializing in the sale of human skulls at $100 per head. He planned to sell the skulls to other business executives like himself, who might find it intriguing to use the product as a conversation piece or a desk ornament. "Death holds a fascination for us mortals," Dashnau claimed. "I've been looking for a way to get rich for many years. . . . If this doesn't do it, nothing will." To date, the idea has not seemed to catch on.

Once rich—or at least comfortable—the main idea seems to be to maintain that enviable condition. Let us not forget one of the richest men ever to live. Andrew Carnegie, who sold his steel corporation for $492,000,000 in 1902, should also be remembered for sharing his wealth. After listening intently to a socialist preach on the injustice of one man possessing so much wealth, and how his finances should be more equitably distributed, Carnegie retired to his study to investigate an even division of his money. After looking up the world's population statistics in his almanac, he instructed his secretary to "give the gentleman $.16. That's his share of my wealth."

Now let us take a look at others who have lived and died, and whose epitaphs evoke the message that "you can't take it with you," even though many of them tried.

Found over the remains of a miser, whose wife did not wish to spend a good deal of money on her husband's tombstone:

"Thorp's Corps."

In commemoration of a well-known miser:
"Here lies one who for medicine would not give
A little gold, and so his life he lost:
I fancy now he'd wish to live again
Could he but guess how much his funeral cost."

In commemoration of a woman who didn't like to pay her debts:

"Here lies the body of our Jean
None in the parish half so mean
She stayed in bed her clothes to save
And nearly drowned to save a grave,
When we all rise on Judgment Day
She'll lie still if there's aught to pay."

Over the tomb of a man whose family's sadness was somewhat cushioned:

"When dear papa went up to Heaven,
What grief mama endured;
And yet that grief was softened,
For papa was insured."

This epitaph deals with the concept of settling the bill of life:

"This world's an Inn, and I her guest;
I've ate and drank and took my rest
With her awhile, and now I pay
Her lavish bill and go my way."

They wept for this fellow, but not for the usual reasons:

"He never won immortal fame
Nor conquered earthly ills
But men weep for him all the same
He always paid his bills."

In memory of a gent who resided in poverty-stricken housing throughout most of his life:

"Here lies Richard Dent
In his last tenement."

The following inscription was discovered over the remains of Jimmy Wyett, who evidently would do just about anything to save money:

"At rest beneath this slab of stone,
Lies stingy Jimmy Wyett.
He died one morning just at ten
And saved a dinner by it."

In memory of an 80-year-old miser, who always watched his purse strings:

"Thin in beard and thick in purse,
Never man beloved worse,
He went to the grave with many a curse,
The devil and he had both one nurse."

In memory of yet another miser:

"Here lieth Sparges
Who died to save charges."

Though no one cared to commemorate this lady's good qualities, she seems to have been worth burying:

"This is the last long resting place
of dear Jemimer's bones;
Her soul ascended into space
amidst our tears and groans.
She was not pleasing to the eye,
nor had she any brain,
And when she talked 'twas through her nose,
which gave her friends much pain.
But still we feel that she was worth
the money that was spent
Upon the coffin and the hearse
(the mourning plumes were lent)."

Over the grave of a millionaire who discovered that money
wasn't quite enough:

> "He thought of course his holdings must
> Admit him to the Heavenly Trust—
> But when he handed in his proxy,
> He found they wanted orthodoxy."

❦ ❦ ❦

Evidently, at one time, this individual had everything
money could buy—only to lose it:

> "Rich born, rich bred, yet Fate adverse
> His wealth and fortune did reverse.
> He lived and died immensely poor
> July the tenth aged ninety-four."

❦ ❦ ❦

This inscription may put you in a wagering mood:

> "Here lies Stephen Rumbold
> He lived to the age of one hundred and one
> Sanguine and strong
> A hundred to one you don't live so long."

❦ ❦ ❦

Floyd was known to have cheated a few of his peers during
his lifetime:

> "Floyd has died and few have sobbed,
> Since had he lived all had been robbed,
> He's paid Dame Nature's debt 'tis said,
> The only one he ever paid.
> Some doubt that he resigned his breath,
> Some vow he's cheated even death.
> If he is buried, then ye Dead, beware,
> Look to your swaddlings, of your shrouds take care,
> Lest Floyd to your coffin should make his way,
> And steal your linen from your mouldering clay."

❦ ❦ ❦

Certainly, there was no love lost by friends and relatives
when old John Racket died:

> "Here lies John Racket
> In his wooden jacket,
> He kept neither horses nor mules;
> He lived like a hog,
> And died like a dog,
> And left all his money to fools."

The following inscription was found on the gravestone of a
money lender from Nova Scotia:

> "Here lies old twenty-five percent.
> The more he had the more he lent.
> The more he had the more he craved,
> Great God, can this poor soul be saved?"

This interesting remembrance was found near Lebanon,
Connecticut:

> "As a stranger she did die,
> In strange lands she doth lie.
> Here by strangers she was laid,
> And her funeral charges paid."

This gentleman placed the blame for his losses precisely
where the blame was due:

> "Here lies the body of Walter Welch, son
> of Michael Welch of Great Shelsley, who left
> him a fine estate in Shelsley, Hartlebury,
> and Arley; who was ruined by three Quakers,
> three lawyers, and a fanatick to help them."

— 8 —

TO YOUR HEALTH

Without a doubt, one of life's greatest hopes is to rid the world of all physical, disabling sicknesses. Yet, though we strive to achieve such a goal, the medical world has uncovered cures for only a small percentage of the ills that invade our bodies. Often, however, both doctors and patients astound the scientific world with bizarre stories of sickness and healing. Such was the case of Dorothy Mae Stevens Anderson.

On the night of February 1, 1951, temperatures in Chicago, Illinois, dropped to 11 degrees below zero. By the time that rescuers discovered Mrs. Anderson, who had passed out in a drunken stupor and lain in an alley all night unprotected, her body temperature had plunged to 64.4 degrees. To complicate matters, her blood and legs had become frozen solid, and her eyeballs had nearly turned to ice. She was rushed to Michael Reese Hospital where doctors had little hope for her survival. Her pulse was barely 12 beats per minute, small breaths were timed at three to every 60 seconds, and there was no measurable blood pressure.

Determined to do what they could, physicians wrapped

Mrs. Anderson's arms and legs in gauze to keep the frozen flesh from chipping away. They administered strong doses of cortisone. Amazingly, just a little over 24 hours after she was admitted, the woman was once again conscious and taking liquids. In a week she was being nourished by solid foods, and her body temperature had come up to a healthy 100.2 degrees. No one in history had ever survived such a catastrophic situation. And, though both of her legs and nine of her fingers had to be amputated, Mrs. Anderson left the hospital in six months time and lived until 1974.

Just prior to her death from tuberculosis in 1915, Leslie Hansell asked to be buried beneath the bright sun. Complying with her last wish, her husband erected an unusual monument in Oakdale Cemetery, Hendersonville, North Carolina. The top of the tomb was constructed of glass and, when Mrs. Hansell was interred, it was hermetically sealed.

A few years later, when cracks appeared in the tomb walls, area residents feared that germs might escape to infect them all. Workmen were hired to reseal the damaged tomb and, in an effort to avoid any possible outbreak of tuberculosis, went so far as to cover the entire tomb with thick tar.

Just a century earlier in America, the "touch of death" was believed to possess curative power, especially for diseases of the skin. In the minds of many physicians, the cure was most effective if the deceased had died violently—preferably by murder or hanging. The touch of the corpse's hand would get rid of "everything from wens and warts to sterility and cancer." Blood from the hanged man, on the other hand, was said to be a certain cure for leprosy.

Furthermore, a strand from the hangman's rope, tucked neatly inside of a hat, would cure a headache.

Hence, the living attempted to avoid health problems by incorporating the powers of the dead. Dirt from a fresh grave, for example, was thought to clear up warts. Heated mold from a grave would cure a stitch—provided the mold was returned to the grave before sunset. And, in the Ozark Mountains, sores, cancer, and syphilis could all be cured by an application of ground bone powder taken from a long-dead corpse.

And so it goes: medical methods and strange beliefs combine to provide some rather bizarre history. The next sampling of health-related epitaphs are equally odd and amusing.

Dame Mary Page, who was buried near Bunhill Fields in 1728, was known for her lengthy illness, though she never complained:

> "In 67 months she was tapped
> 66 times. Had taken
> away from her 240 gallons of
> water—without ever repining
> at her case."

This curious epitaph was found over the grave of a man from Fosbrooke, Northumberland:

> "Here lieth Matthew Hollingshead,
> Who died from cold caught in his head.
> It brought on fever and rheumatiz,
> Which ended me—for here I is."

A likeable doctor from Pawtucket, Rhode Island, who had made it a habit to foot the medical bills of many of his patients, inscribed his own epitaph on a large boulder. Today, it marks his grave in Oak Grove Cemetery:

> "William P. Rothwell M.D.
> 1866–1939
> This is on me."

No warning of impending doom was given to David Gardiner, according to his stone in the Ancient Burying Ground, Hartford, Connecticut:

"Well—sick—dead in one hour's space."

🍎 🍎 🍎

Over the remains of a young girl, who died a mysterious death in New Jersey:

"Julia Adams
Died of *thin shoes*,
April 17th, 1839
aged 19 years."

🍎 🍎 🍎

A thought-provoking memory of a woman who had one bad leg:

"Here lies Dame Dorothy Peg,
Who never had issue except in her leg,
So great was her art, so deep was her cunning,
That while one leg stood, the other kept running."

🍎 🍎 🍎

Obviously, the family of Frances Cerny, who was buried in St. Mary's Cemetery, Winona, Minnesota, did not feel that their daughter had died of natural causes:

"Killed by unskilled Dr."

🍎 🍎 🍎

On the tombstone of a woman who was grossly overweight:

"All flesh is grass,
The scriptures they do say,
And grass when dead
Is turned into hay.
Now when the reaper her away do take
My what a wopping haystack she will make."

This amusing epitaph was inscribed over the tomb of an overweight woman:

"Constance Bevon, wife of John
Lies beneath this marble stone;
Fat and busom, round and stout,
'Twas apoplexy bowled her out."

In memory of Roger Morton, who should have been a mite more careful:

"Here lies entombed one Robert Morton,
Whose sudden death was early brought on;
Trying one day his corn to mow off,
The razor slipped, and cut his toe off;
The toe, or, rather, what it grew to,
An inflammation quickly flew to;
The parts, they took to mortifying,
And poor dear Roger, he took to dying."

Obviously, the parents of young Jonathan Tute, aged 14, laid to rest in North Cemetery, Vernon, Vermont blamed the doctors who had treated him:

"But tho' his Spirit fled on high
His body mould'ring here must lie
Behold the amazing alteration
Effected by Inoculation
The means employed his life to save
Hurried him headlong into the grave."

Over a pair of identical twins who were born prematurely:

"Two lovelier babes ye nare did see
Than Providence did give to me,
But they was took with ague fits
And here they lie as dead as nits."

Over the remains of Molly Dickie, the loving wife of Hall Dickie, a tailor:

"Two great physicians first
My loving husband tried,
To cure my pain—
In vain,
At last he got a third,
And then I died."

Undoubtedly, according to the inscription over the remains of Ruth Sprague, in Maple Grove Cemetery, Hoosick Falls, New York, physicians were once believed to be an "evil" lot:

"She was stolen from the grave
by Roderick R. Clow & dissected
at Dr. P. M. Armstrong's office
in Hoosick, N.Y. from which place
her mutilated remains were
obtained and deposited here.
Her body dissected by fiendish men
Her bones anatomised,
Her soul we trust has risen to God
Where few physicians rise."

The following was, without a doubt, a strange way to try to cure Mrs. McFadden:

"Mrs. McFadden has gone from this life;
She has left all its sorrows and cares;
She caught the rheumatics in both of her legs,
While scrubbing the cellar and stairs.
They put mustard plasters upon her in vain;
They bathed her with whiskey and rum;
But Thursday her spirit departed, and left
Her body entirely numb."

There's something to be said for the warning, "Don't drink the water," as proven by this inscription in a Cheltenham churchyard:

> "Here lies I and my two daughters,
> Killed by drinking Cheltenham waters;
> If we had stuck to Epsom salts,
> We shouldn't be lying in these here vaults."

❦ ❦ ❦

Though it uses poor English, this epitaph discovered in an aging cemetery near Bangor, Maine, gets its point across:

> "Poor Martha Snell, her's gone away,
> Her would if her could, but her couldn't stay,
> Her had two bad legs and a badish cough,
> But her legs it was that carried her off."

❦ ❦ ❦

Forever known as a man of few words, Dr. J. J. Subers had the following epitaph placed on his tombstone, which stands in Rosehill Cemetery, Macon, Georgia:

> "Been Here
> and Gone
> Had A Good Time."

❦ ❦ ❦

An epitaph that is inscribed on a worn stone near Yorkshire speaks of tight clothes:

> "Mary had a little waist,
> She laced it smaller still;
> A stone o'er Mary has been placed
> Upon this silent hill.

> And on this stone these words are writ,
> 'Oh, let us hope she's gone,
> Where angels never care a bit
> 'Bout what they have got on.' "

❦ ❦ ❦

One inscription, found in Tennessee, warns of expecting the seasons to change too early:

> "Beneath this stone, a lump of clay,
> Lies Uncle Peter Dan'els,
> Who, early in the month of May,
> Took off his winter flannels."

Apparently, a lack of patience led to the death of Mary Ann Lowder, who is buried in Burlington, Vermont:

> "Here lies the body of Mary Ann Lowder,
> She burst while drinking a seidlitz powder,
> Called from this world to her heavenly rest,
> She should have waited till it effervesced."

Actually, we doubt that this woman could have possibly weighed that much:

> "Beneath this monumental stone
> Lies half a ton of flesh and bone."

The following is certainly a unique comparison:

> "Collisions sore, three, four, she bore
> Physicians were in vain,
> For old and rusted the boil busted
> And smashed the excursion train.
> Her end was in pieces."

Evidently, in the case of George Augustus Clough, who died of syphilis and was buried in St. Michael's Churchyard, Charleston, South Carolina, a less direct term was used to describe his affliction:

> "Died suddenly of Stranger's fever."

The following blunt opinion is found in Oasis Cemetery, near West Branch, Iowa, over the remains of two children, Ralph and John Akers:

> "Let medical science loom up
> High as it will
> The order of Quacks
> Will stick to it still."

On Dr. Thomas Fossett's tombstone, in the Unitarian Church, Barnstable, Massachusetts, we find a bit of boasting:

> "I have practiced on the eclectic
> system in Mass., Ohio and Mich.,
> for over 50 years and have never lost that number of
> patients."

Do you get the feeling they never pinpointed the real cause of this lady's death?:

> "Of pneumonia supervening consumption,
> complicated with other diseases, the
> main symptom of which was insanity."

The following tombstone was restored by a garrison of U.S. soldiers long after the Revolutionary War:

> "An honest soldier never is forgot,
> Whether he die by musket or by pot."

The following was written by relieved family members over the body of a man who froze to death:

> "The winter snow congealed his form,
> But now we know our uncle's warm."

How long did this woman, who was buried near Bayfield, Mississippi, actually hope to live?

> "Stranger, pause, my tale attend,
> And learn the cause of Hannah's end.
> Across the world the wind did blow,
> She ketched a cold that laid her low.
> We shed a lot of tears 'tis true,
> But life is short—aged 82."

In memory of an aging prisoner, who died while incarcerated at Gray's Inn Lane Workhouse:

> "Old Jerry's dead at last (God rest his soul)
> His body's shoveled down some work-house hole,
> Or else to doctors given for dissection.
> His spirit has gone to Old Nick for correction,
> And his old clothes to spread some new infection."

This inscription, no longer very legible, can be found in Pleasant Grove Cemetery, Ithaca, New York:

> "While on earth my knee was lame,
> I had to nurse and heed it.
> But now I've gone to a better place
> Where I do not even need it."

Gee, what happens to the time?

> "She was in health at 11:30 A.M.
> And left for Heaven at 3:30 P.M."

Sometimes, there is too much time, as in this sad epitaph:

> "The pale consumption gave the fatal blow,
> The fate was certain although the event was slow."

The following inscription, perhaps, gives too much credit to 79 hours of suffering:

"Died, on the 14th inst., Henry Wilkins
Gly, aged 3 days and 7 hours. After a
long and painful illness, which he bore
with Christian fortitude, this youthful
martyr departed to his rest."

In memory of a child, who didn't heed warnings of smoking:

"Little Johnny Day lies here
He neither fumes nor frets.
He had just reached his thirteenth year—
Cigarettes."

9

HEAVEN AND HELL

The twin concepts of heaven and hell have fascinated mankind since the earliest recorded history. The classic portrait of them has in modern times come to appear a bit outdated even in the minds of true believers, and few clergymen continue to describe one as a place of "angels, harps, and halos," and the other as an "underground inferno." However, they and their followers do, indeed, subscribe to the ideal of a life in the hereafter. Though they do not pinpoint exactly what to expect, numerous people have suggested a means of getting to the good place.

On February 29, 1736, in Manchester, England, Ann Lee was born, who was destined to become known as the "second incarnation of Christ." In 1762, she married a blacksmith named Abraham Standerin and together, they bore four children, each of whom died in infancy. From that point on, Ann Lee travelled throughout the country preaching against sexual intercourse, which she referred to as "filthy gratification" that would inevitably lead to "a covenant with death and an agreement with hell." In the afterlife, she warned, those who participated in this, the "root of all depravity," would be tied up and tortured.

In 1774, along with eight disciples, she emigrated to the United States, where she settled in Waterliet, New York. Anyone who came to live in that colony was expected to practice complete celibacy and communal ownership of property. By the practice of adopting orphan children, the religious sect, which became known as the "Shaking Quakers," grew in size. And "Mother Ann," as she was now known, won other new converts as well until her death in 1783. By 1826, there were 18 Shaker communities from Maine to Indiana. Today, only one active group survives.

On the opposite end of heavenly salvation, we find theologian Theophilus Gates, who was the father (in more ways than one) of a strange religious sect known in history as the "Battle Axes." The center of his worship was the Shenkel Reform Church, a formidable stone and stucco building erected near Pottstown, Pennsylvania, in 1838. Here, Gates and his congregation were known for their unorthodox prayer meetings, which were held in the nude.

While working as a freelance writer of religious prophecy, Gates met Hannah Williamson, who joined him in his venture of selling copies of the *Battle Axe* story. Together, they founded the church in Shenkel to propagate their erotic visions of worship. Gathering together nearly 50 men and women, the Battle Axe congregation would shed its clothes and exercise religious freedom beyond the imaginations of most hedonists. Any member, man or woman, had the privilege of visiting another member's home, claiming to have heard the Heavenly Voice, and absconding with the neighbor's spouse.

Gates' extraordinary beliefs did not end there. Once, convinced that the best way to reach heaven was to "fly," he donned a pair of homemade wings and flapped off a second-story rooftop; it took him almost a month to recover from his injuries.

The last that was known of the Battle Axe movement was

that they were continuing to flourish. After all, could the Catholics or Baptists claim such happy churchgoers? Inevitably, though area residents persistently harassed the congregation, Gates' members shed still further inhibitions, allegedly enjoying one another's mates in the aisles of the Shenkel church.

Ethan Allen, a well-known American hero and professed atheist, attended a Calvinist church ceremony late in life in order to reinforce his own beliefs. The sermon that day touched upon heaven, with the minister proclaiming that "many shall strive to enter in, but shall not be able." When the preacher went on to say that only one out of 80 would be allowed to enter the kingdom of Heaven, Allen grabbed his hat and walked toward the door, saying "I'm off, boys—any one of you may take my chance. . . ."

"Oh, the harlots!" exclaimed Reverend John McDowall in his diary. He had just completed his first soul-saving trip into New York City's seamiest district in 1830, and he was intent on bringing "moral and religious improvement" to the entire urban area. Reverend McDowall spent considerable time meeting with pimps, whores, and thieves, bombarding them with intense sermons on the damnation of hell, and even inducing one or two fallen women to quit the world's oldest profession.

Over the period of several months, McDowall gathered information on many of New York's corrupt corners. Eventually, he published a detailed account of the lurid corruption he had found in a pamphlet entitled *McDowall's Journal.* For every Christian living within New York city limits, it seemed there was another that called the Reverend a "pornographer." In reality, McDowall's booklet was a fairly hot item, for it gave spicy accounts of, among others, "Tahitian maidens brought to New York to work as prostitutes," and contained a complete list of bordellos. In the end, McDowall's work became known as the "Whorehouse Directory," and it was the best-selling pamphlet of the decade.

Hence, to those who came before us, the salvation of heaven and damnation of hell took many forms. Here is a sampling of quaint epitaphs that deals with this inevitable, unavoidable disposition of the soul.

It seems obvious where the friends and relatives of this man believed his destination to be:
"John burns."

Inscribed on a narrow gravestone in Wellsboro, Pennsylvania:
"Daniel E. Cole
Born Feb. 2, 1844
Went Away
Mar. 22, 1921
I wonder
Where he went."

Which way did they go—which way did they go?
"Here is Mr. Dudley senior, and Jane his wife also;
Who while living was his superior, but see what death can do.
Two of his sons also lie here, one Walter, t'other Joe:
They all of them went—in the year 1510—below."

In Harmony, Rhode Island, we find the tombstone of Emma Luther, who wasn't quite sure whether or not there was a place called Heaven, but covered all her bases:
"If there is another world
I live in bliss
If not another
I have made the most of this. . . ."

Found over the remains of Andrew Meekie, whose reputation was not so hot—but his destination was:

> "Beneath these stones lie Meekie's bones:
> Oh! Satan can you take him,
> Appoint him tutor to your weans
> And clever devils he'll make 'em."

Still another question concerning future destination was expressed on a monument commemorating Charles A. Miller, in Siloam Cemetery, Vineland, New Jersey:

> "I came I know not whence,
> I go I know not whither."

The person who composed this epitaph hoped that there was a roped-off place for folks like Ellen Hill:

> "This is to the memory of Ellen Hill
> A woman who could always have her will.
> She snubbed her husband and she made good bread
> Yet on the whole he's rather glad she's dead.
> She whipped her children and she drank her gin,
> Whipped virtue out and whipped the devil in.
> May all such women go to some great fold
> Where they through all eternity may scold."

Into the tombstone of Rodney Webber, in Rural Cemetery, Virgil, New York, is etched a finger pointing upward toward the skies, below which reads:

> "He's gone home."

A dubious one-word inscription appears on the tombstone of Lorenzo Sabine, who was buried in Eastport, Maine:

> "Transplanted"

It seems no one had anything good to say about Coleman:
> "If heaven be pleased when sinners cease to sin,
> If hell be pleased when sinners enter in,
> If earth be pleased when ridded of a knave,
> Then all are pleased, for Coleman's in his grave."

In memory of a father, who went to make reservations:
> "Our papa dear has gone to Heaven
> To make arrangements for eleven."

This intriguing epitaph makes a comparison between losing a family member and banking:
> "Our first deposit in Heaven."

Evidently, the devil was going to eat well that night:
> "Here lies the carcass
> Of a cursed sinner,
> Doomed to be roasted,
> For the Devil's dinner."

Found over the remains of Ebenezer Dockwood:
> "Ebenezer Dockwood
> Aged forty-seven,
> A miser and a hypocrite,
> And never went to heaven."

The following commemoration proved her parent's perception of their "perfect" daughter:
> "God hath chosen her as a pattern for the other
> Angels."

When this lady died, she left her loved one *forever*:
"She died, poor dear, of disappointed love,
And angels bore her soul to realms above.
When her young man is summoned, so they say,
He will be carried off the other way."

The following misspelled inscription was found near Germantown, Pennsylvania:
"Here lies the dust of Louisa Orr, whose soul is now a
little *angle* in Heaven."

Remembering a man who "jined" every group and organization while he was alive:
"Mason, Elk, and Mystic Shriner—
Georgie was a steady jiner,
He jined what e'er a jiner should,
He jined most everything he could.

He jined the good, he jined the ill,
It's safe to say he's jining still—
Where he has gone, we do not know,
Perhaps he's jining things below."

The epitaph on a weathered slate stone in Old North Cemetery, Nantucket, Massachusetts, was barely legible:
"Under the sod
Under these trees
Lies the body of Jonathan Pease
He is not here
But only his pod
He has shelled out his peas
And gone to his God."

This brief epitaph deals neatly with what we know about life after death:

> "What I was once some may relate,
> What I am now is each one's fate;
> What I shall be none can explain,
> Till he that called, call again."

🐛 🐛 🐛

Certainly, this man discovered that "seeing the light" isn't always something to look forward to:

> "Beneath this plain pine board is lying the body of
> Joshua Hight,
> 'Cheer up,' the parson told him, dying:
> 'Your future's very bright,'
>
> Slowly the sick man raised his head,
> His weeping friends amazing.
> 'Parson, it's most too bright,' he said,
> 'For I can see it blazing!' "

🐛 🐛 🐛

These friends and neighbors were, quite obviously, grieving for both Mary Anne *AND* Abraham:

> "Mary Anne has gone to rest,
> Safe at last on Abraham's breast,
> Which may be nuts for Mary Anne,
> But is certainly rough on Abraham."

🐛 🐛 🐛

The following was discovered on a weathered tombstone in a small country cemetery near Grafton, Vermont:

> "Gone Home Below"

Confused by his true destination, the man's widow added the following announcement:

> "To follow you I'm not content.
> Unless I know which way you went."

🐛 🐛 🐛

In memory of a good Marine officer:
>"Here lies retired from busy scenes
>A First Lieutenant of Marines;
>Who lately lived in peace and plenty
>On board the ship the Atalanti:
>Now, stripped of all his warlike show,
>And laid in box of elm below,
>Confined to earth in narrow borders
>He rises not till further orders."

No one seems to be anxious to follow this lady:
>"Now she is dead and cannot stir
>Her cheeks are like a faded rose.
>Which one of us must follow her
>The Lord Almighty only knows."

Maybe there's another place?
>"Too bad for Heaven, too good for Hell,
>So, where he's gone, I cannot tell."

Though it seems odd, here's a piece of advice from Martin
Elmerod for God:
>"Here lies Martin Elmerod.
>Have mercy on my soul, good God
>As I would do were I Lord God
>And you were Martin Elmerod."

She got recalled:
>"Here rests a fine woman which was sent from above
>To teach virtues and graces to men.
>But God when he saw her in such very bad hands
>Recalled her to Heaven again."

This extensive sermon about heaven and hell was discovered over the grave of Messenger Monsey, aged 96 when he died:

"Here lie my old limbs, my vexation now ends,
For I've lived much too long for myself and my friends;
As for churchyards and grounds which parsons call
Holy,
'Tis a rank piece of priestcraft and founded in folly;
In short, I despise them; and as for my soul,
Which may mount the last day with my bones from this
hole,
I think that I really hath nothing to fear
From the God of mankind, whom I truly revere;
What the next world may be, little troubles my pate;
If not better than this, I beseech thee, oh Fate,
When the bodies of millions fly up in a riot
To let the old carcass of Monsey be quiet."

A two-word epitaph, dedicated to Arthur Haine in City Cemetery, Vancouver, Washington, recalls a bonafide and stubborn atheist:

"Haine Haint."

10

ODD PRACTICES AND STRANGE HABITS

Odd practices and strange habits are often remembered long after a person dies. Therefore, it seems only fitting that a great number of people are laid to rest and commemorated with epitaphs that recall these peculiar inclinations. Such was the case of Reuben Smith, who wanted to be buried sitting up.

Reuben died in 1899 at the age of 71 in Amesbury, Massachusetts. Prior to his death, he requested that he be buried in Mt. Prospect Cemetery, seated comfortably in a chair next to a table. Furthermore, he wanted his favorite pipe, a newspaper, and a checkerboard to be situated on top of the table in front of him. But that wasn't Smith's only unusual request. Oddly enough, the eccentric gentleman offered a substantial amount of his wealth to any woman who would be willing to spend a night with his corpse in the tomb. Explaining Smith's strange desire, the *Amesbury Daily News* wrote the following commentary on January 25, 1899:

"Arrangements for the funeral of the late Reuben Smith have been perfected. The body will be laid out in the reclining chair as directed by Mr. Smith and will be taken to the Mt. Prospect cemetery in that condition by Undertaker Austin. Agreeable to Mr. Smith's desire (of having a woman spend the night in) the tomb, a costly one of his own design, will be left open an hour for public inspection after the body is placed there, when the door will be bricked up. Mr. Smith made arrangements with Mr. Austin about two weeks before his death and told him where the key to the tomb was. . . ."

It is unknown whether or not any enterprising lady took Mr. Smith up on his proposal.

Though his request was unusual, Reuben Smith was not the only person who wanted to be buried in an upright position. Britt Bailey, who died in 1832, wanted no one to be able to say, "Here lies Britt Bailey." Hence, he was buried on his own property, in Brazoria County, Texas—standing up. Furthermore, as a traveller who explored the West extensively, he asked that his face be turned towards the setting sun.

Strangely, every once in a while, it is reported that an unexplainable light arises from the area where "Britt Bailey stands." After floating about the countryside, the light returns to the same spot and disappears. The spectacle, known locally as "Bailey's Light," is believed to be Bailey's ghost rising on occasion to search for a man who stole a jug of whiskey from his grave.

The last will and testament of Sarah E. Griffiths, who died in 1887, said in part that her executor should provide "a suitable monument and fit up the lot." The executor interpreted this to mean that Sarah wanted her entire vast fortune to be spent on her monument. Therefore, over her remains, which were interred in the private Griffiths Cemetery near Newmarket, New Hampshire, stands a huge tombstone in her memory.

Angered, Mrs. Griffiths' sole heir erected a miniature stone for himself. On its face he carved a hand pointing in the direction of the towering memorial, and wrote:
"A Suitable Monument
and fit up the lot. S.E.G."

❦ ❦ ❦

Finally, let us remember Evelyn Price, a youngster who just loved to dance. By the age of five, she had become rather famous for her habitual toe-tapping, and all who knew her personally appreciated her talents. Sadly, young Evelyn died in 1922 at the tender age of six. She was buried in Aspen Grove Cemetery, Burlington, Iowa, beneath a curious, conversation-inducing monument: a glassed-in box, filled with newspaper clippings of the child's dancing exploits.

Some have come and gone in this world who were famous for their odd practices and their annoying, sometimes intrusive, habits—some were loved or respected for them. The following epitaphs relate these actions in concrete, marble, and slate.

❦ ❦ ❦

A family monument in Elgin, Minnesota, indicates disapproval of political practices:
"None of us ever voted for
Roosevelt or Truman."

❦ ❦ ❦

Evidently, Sir John Plumpudding felt that he needed some excitement in his life:
"Here lies Sir John Plumpudding
of the Grange,
Who hanged himself one morning
for a change."

A quaint memory of a talkative old maid:
> "Beneath this silent stone is laid
> A noisy, antiquated maid,
> Who from her cradle talked till death,
> And never before was out of breath."

And still another who died on May Day:
> "Here lies, returned to clay
> Miss Arabella Young,
> Who on the first of May
> Began to hold her tongue."

Over the body of a lady who, without a doubt, lived in the fast lane:
> "Josephine lies here below,
> Upon my word, she was not slow,
> The life she led was very sporty—
> She died when she was nearly forty."

Habitually, it seems, Charles H. Petty was determined to stay clean, no matter what the risk:
> "His death occurred in nine hours
> after being bitten by a shark,
> while bathing near the ship."

The following inscription, found in East Cemetery, near Marlboro, New Hampshire, commemorates the seemingly pointless life's work of Daniel Emerson:
> "The land I cleared is now my grave
> Think well my friends how you behave."

The ethical integrity of a lawyer named Charles Elliot, who is buried in the Christ Episcopal Churchyard, New Bern, North Carolina, was upheld by his epitaph—or was it?

"An honest lawyer indeed."

Evidently, attorney John E. Goembel was in the habit of arguing with both of his wives:

"The Defense Rests."

The following inscription was found in Saratoga, New York, over the remains of a wife who habitually avoided sleeping with her husband:

"Here lies the wife of Robert Ricular,
Who walked the way of God perpendicular."

Mathies G. Braden, who was buried in Old Manden Cemetery, near Bismarck, North Dakota, was married to a woman who found happiness in the most somber places:

"Stranger call this not a place
Of Fear and Gloom.
To me it is a Pleasant Spot,
It is my Husbands tomb."

Though H. Amanzo Dygert was, apparently, involved in everything else, he was not involved in marriage:

"An American by birth
A German Dutchman by descent
A Republican in Politics
A Congregationalist in Religion
A Druggist by Profession
A Batchelor by fate."

The following fitting epitaph was dedicated to William Wilson, who had the annoying habit of being a chronic complainer:

"Here lieth W. W.
Who never more will trouble you, trouble you."

The tombstone of another gent, who was a habitual liar:

"Here lies a man who while he lived
Was happy as a linnet.
He always lied while on the earth
And now he's lying in it."

As far as everyday actions were concerned, this woman was predictable:

"For three score years this life Cleora led,
At morn she rose, at night she went to bed."

In memory of a young woman who remained untouched until the day she died:

"Here lies poor Charlotte,
Who was no harlot,
But in her virginity
Though just turned nineteen—
Which within this vicinity,
Is hard to be found and seen."

Though Martha may have been a tease, she eventually had to capitulate:

"Here lieth the body of Martha Dias,
Always noisy, not very pious,
Who lived to the age of three score and ten,
And gave to worms what she refused to men."

Mr. Cordes, who resided near North East, Maryland, regularly beat his wife. After she died of abuse, he married again, this time to Annie. Annie was laid to rest in the Bethel Methodist Churchyard with the following telling words upon her gravestone:

"Hard to beat."

This remembrance, which condemns by omission, is found in the Hill Burying Ground, Concord, Massachusetts:

"She was very Excellent for Reading & Soberness"

Thomas Gilbert, laid to rest in Hadley Cemetery, East Hampstead, New Hampshire, felt that a number of people ruined him financially and was not above naming names:

"Beneath this stone is grave for one
Shamefully robbed in life
By his wife's son and Squire Tom
And Daniel Seavey's wife."

She made a habit of doing things on Thursday:

"On a Thursday she was born,
On a Thursday made a bride,
On a Thursday put to bed,
On a Thursday broke her leg,
On a Thursday died."

Eunice Page, who was buried in Plainfield, Vermont, only had two practices in life and both seem to have been tiresome:

"Five time five years I lived a virgin's life
Nine times five years I lived a virtuous wife,
Wearied of this mortal life, I rest."

The following inscription, in commemoration to Mary Bond, is probably the most descriptive epitaph ever written:

"Here lie the bodies
of Thomas Bond and Mary his wife
She was temperate, chaste, and charitable
BUT
She was proud, peevish and passionate.
She was an affectionate wife, and a tender mother
BUT
Her husband and her child whom she loved
Seldom saw her countenance without a disgusting frown,
Whilst she received visitors whom she despised
With an endearing smile.
Her behavior was discreet toward strangers
BUT
Independent to her family.
Abroad her conduct was influenced by good breeding
BUT
At home, by ill temper.
She was a professed enemy to flattery,
And was seldom known to praise or command,
BUT
The talents in which she principally excelled,
Were difference of opinion and discovering flaws
And imperfections.
BUT
She was an admirable economist,
And, with prodigality,
Dispensed plenty to every person in her family:
BUT
Would sacrifice their eyes to a farthing candle.
She sometimes made her husband happy with her
Good qualities;
BUT
Much more frequently miserable—with her many
failings
Insomuch that in 30 years cohabitation

He often lamented all her virtues,
He had not in the whole enjoyed two years of
Matrimonial comfort,
BUT
AT LENGTH
Finding that she had lost the affection of her husband,
As well as the regard of her neighbours,
Family disputes having been divulged by servants,
She died of vexation, July 20, 1768,
Aged 48 years.
BUT
Her worn-out husband survived her four months and
two days,
And departed this life Nov. 28, 1768,
In the 54th year of his age.
FURTHER
William Bond brother to the deceased erected this stone
As a weekly monitor, to the surviving wives of this
parish,
That they may avoid the infamy of having their
memories
handed to posterity
With a PATCH WORK character."

Over the remains of a woman who may be supposed to
have had a number of intimate encounters:
"On this marble drop a tear,
Here lies fair Rosalind;
All mankind was pleased with her,
And she with all mankind."

To Mary Ann Andrews, buried in Christian Churchyard,
Conklingville, New York, an ambiguous statement:
"She hath done what she could."

She remained virginal all her life—but not by choice:
> "Tis true I led a single life
> And ne'er was married in my life,
> For of that sex I ne'er had none:
> It is the Lord: his will be done."

Briefly, an inscription in East Calais, Vermont, leaves us with a clear picture of this gentleman's habits:
> "P. S.
> The Old Nuisance"

Words were not wasted on the tombstone of Deacon Lemuel Willard, in Harvard, Massachusetts:
> "When present useful;
> Absent, wanted.
> Lived, respected.
> Died, Lamented."

An epitaph in Norway, Maine, says it all about Asa Barton:
> "His faults are buried
> with him beneath this
> stone. His virtues
> (if he had any) are
> remembered by his friends."

Over the tomb of a gentleman who was a skeptic about nearly everything:
> "I was not
> I am not
> I grieve not."

This man's hobby, in Alston, Cumberland, was bone collecting:

"Here lies poor Jones,
Who all his life collected bones;
But death, that great and grisly spectre,
That most amazing bone collector,
Hath boned poor Jones, so neat and tidy,
That here he lies in bona-fide."

Etched into the tomb of a beer brewer from New Jersey, who seems to have taken the major ingredient with him:

"Here lies poor Burton,
He was both hale and stout;
Death laid him on his bitter beer,
Now in another world he *hops* about."

In memory of a man named Fred, whose habit it was to sleep his life away:

"Here lie the bones of Foolish Fred:
Who wasted precious time in bed,
A fellow hit him on the head—
And thanks be praised—our Freddie's dead.

11

MIXED MEMORIES

There remains a hodgepodge of tombstone inscriptions scattered throughout the world that fall into no specific categories. Yet, the stories behind them are a very real piece of humanity that can be translated in a great number of ways.

Such as the case of a headstone standing in Fort Gibson National Cemetery, Oklahoma, which long represented a mystery. Although it can clearly be seen with the one-word inscription of "Vivia," for decades no one really knew who Vivia was. In actuality, she was the loving sweetheart of a soldier stationed at Fort Gibson. To be close to him, she disguised herself as a soldier and sneaked onto the base. Her sex went undiscovered until after her death, when disturbed officials were unsure what they should do with her remains. In the end, she was buried without the true facts being mentioned.

The tombstone over the Reverend William Richardson, in Waxhaw Presbyterian Churchyard, near Lancaster,

South Carolina, fails to mention the mysterious circumstances of his death or the macabre method used to detect
foul play. Richardson was discovered in his chambers in a
kneeling position, a bridle tightly drawn around his throat.
Whether he had been murdered or had taken his own life
could not be determined.

Later in the year, however, when the Reverend's volup-
tuous, young widow married George Dunlop, parishioners
became suspicious. They charged her with killing her husband, exhumed his body, and forced her to lay her hands
on the decomposed corpse. It was, at that time, believed
that blood would flow from any victim who was touched by
his or her murderer. Though the ordeal was, undoubtedly,
emotionally scarring to Richardson's widow, the results
were inconclusive. She was found innocent of any wrong-
doing.

S. P. Dinsmoor, of Lucas, Kansas, died in 1932 at the age
of 89. Before that fateful day, however, Dinsmoor had
spent years building his own tomb. Using no less than
2,273 bags of cement, he constructed a two-story house; a
cement tree of life that is guarded by an angel; a cement
devil situated high in another cement tree; cement images
of Adam and Eve; and, indeed, a cement evil serpent.
Within the monument, which rises 40 feet into the air, are
a pair of cement coffins, one for himself and one for his
wife. On top of his coffin is a plate-glass lid that serves two
distinct purposes, as explained by Dinsmoor before he
died:

> "I have a will that none except my wife, my
> descendants, their husbands and wives, shall go to
> see me for less than $1. That will pay some one to
> look after the place, and I promise everyone that
> comes in to see me (they can look through the plate
> glass and . . . see my face) that if I see them
> dropping a dollar in the hands of the flunky, and I
> see the dollar, I will give them a smile."

At the foot of his coffin Dinsmoor positioned a two-gallon, cement jug, and wrote:

"In the resurrection morn, if I have to go
below, I'll grab my jug and fill it with water on
the road down. They say they need water down below."

There just wasn't much to be said about the life of John Shore, except for the fact that he did, indeed, live at one time:

"Here lies John Shore
I say no more
Who was alive
In sixty-five."

Obviously, this aging woman, buried in a rural Maryland graveyard, was prone to forgetfulness:

"Elizabeth Scott lies buried here.
She was born Nov. 20th, 1785,
according to the best of her recollection."

A marble cutter, without sufficient room on the headstone for the intended message, wrote:

"Let her R.I.P."

When this tombstone was erected, John Eldred was not yet quite prepared to be buried:

"Here lies the body of John Eldred,
At least he will be here when he is dead;
But now at this time he is alive
The 14th of August, Sixty-Five."

Evidently, by the time this tombstone was erected in Necropolis, Glasgow, grieving friends had forgotten where Bess Bell was buried:

"Here lies Bess Bell,
But whereabouts I cannot tell."

A patriotic occurrence might have been lost to the annals of history if it weren't for the tombstone of Rebecca Jones, who was buried in Pleasant Grove Cemetery, near Raleigh, North Carolina:

"Devoted Christian mother who whipped
Sherman's bummers with scalding water
while trying to take her dinner pot
which contained a ham bone being
cooked for her soldier boys."

Evidently, John Decatur Barry, who was buried in Oakdale Cemetery, Wilmington, North Carolina, grew some with the passage of time:

"I found him a pigmy,
And left him a giant."

An epitaph that was obviously misspelled; or was it?

"Great his our grief
Great was her pain,
Great his our loss
Great his her gain."

Over the remains of one who was not prepared:

"Grim death took me without any warning,
I was well at night, and dead at nine in the morning."

The author worked hard to make this epitaph rhyme:
> "Ingenious youth, thou art laid in dust,
> Thy friends, for thee, in tears did bust."

Over the remains of a man whose body was discovered after it had become ossified:
> "He died hard."

Though the parents of this youngster used poor grammar, it is the thought that counts:
> "Little Willie, he was our lily,
> God for him sent, and we let him went."

Obviously, his most cherished desire was to be laid to rest forever looking up:
> "Here I at length repose
> My spirit now at aise is;
> With the tips of my toes
> And the point of my nose
> Turned up to the roots of the daisies."

Those who wrote the following epitaph on the tombstone of Jonathan Richardson, in East Thompson, Connecticut, seem to have got the story a bit twisted:
> "Here lies one who never sacrificed his
> reason at the altar of superstitious
> God, who never believed that Jonah
> swallowed the whale."

In commemoration of a cranky, old man:
> "Deeply regretted by all who never knew him."

There just wasn't much to be said for poor Ned:
"Here lies Ned,
There is nothing more to be said—
Because we like to speak well of the dead."

Strange Creek, West Virginia, is named for William Strange, who became hopelessly lost while out on a surveying expedition. His bleached bones were discovered several years later, near his rifle, which continued to lean against a tree. On the bark, Strange had carved his own epitaph:
"Strange is my name and I'm on Strange ground
And Strange it is I can't be found."

In the opinion of his friends, it wouldn't do any good to give John a second chance:
"Here lies John Hill,
A man of skill,
Whose age was five times ten:
He never did good
And never would
If he lived as long again."

This curious memory was etched upon the tombstone of a man who was cremated:
"The soul has flown
And the body's flue."

In memory of a baby, who apparently didn't like what he saw:
"He came to see the farce of life one day,
Tired of the first act, and so went away."

She possessed something more than a green thumb:
"The pretty flowers that blossom here
Are fertilized by Gertie Greer."

What was that again?
"Sacred to twins Charlie and Varlie
Sons of loving parents who died in infancy."

The following inscription, discovered on the tombstone of Edward Oakes in West Cemetery, Middlebury, Vermont, has an interesting double meaning:
"Faithful husband thou art
At rest until we meet again."

A brief, conflicting message was found on this tombstone:
"Sacred to the memory of *three* twins."

In both life and in death, Silas W. Sanderson, justice of the Supreme Court, had the last word:
"Final Decree."

When Colonel William L. Saunders, Secretary of State in North Carolina, was questioned by a Congressional committee on his connections with the Ku Klux Klan, he refused to answer. Apparently, his refusal to cooperate was never forgotten, for his epitaph reads:
"I decline to answer."

Over the grave of a man whose body was apparently snatched from St. Mark's Churchyard in New York City:
"He is not here."

James Collins, whose wife was buried in Caribou, Colorado, seems to have been advertising for another mate and mother for his children:

> "Sarah Collins,
> Gone before us O our Sister
> To the spirit land
> Vainly look we for another,
> in thy place to stand."

This man, who buried his wife in Little Compton, Rhode Island, felt that he had married the wrong woman, for standing side-by-side are two stones which read:

"In memory of	"In Memory of
Elizabeth who	Lidia ye Wife of
should have been	Mr. Simeon Palmer"
the wife of	
Mr. Simeon Palmer"	

Either the man who cut this stone made another mistake— or it just *felt* like 708 years:

> "Here lyeth the BOdy of Mrs. ANIIE SMITH,
> WhO dePartED thiS Life OCtO the 28, in the
> yeare 1701.
> Shee LiVed a Maid And died aged 708."

Eugene Gladstone O'Neill, the famous playwright, died in a Boston hotel room in 1953, and was buried in Forest Hills Cemetery, Jamaica Plain, Massachusetts. Though there is no epitaph adorning his tombstone, executors might have inscribed his final words:

> "I knew it, I knew it!
> Born in a goddam hotel room and dying in a hotel
> room!"

This misleading epitaph is found in Felchville, Vermont:
"On the 31st of Aug., 1754, Capt. James
Johnson had a daughter born on this spot of
ground, being *captivated* with his whole family
by the Indians."

Evidently, the stonecutter for this tomb was hard-pressed
to find a good rhyme:
"Here lies Sir John Hawkins,
Without his shoes or his stawkins."

Over a gentleman who committed suicide in France, we
find this humorous reasoning:
"Tired of this eternal buttoning
and unbuttoning."

The man who composed this epitaph seemed to know sev-
eral women intimately:
"The dame that rests beneath this tomb
Had Rachel's beauty, Leah's fruitful womb,
Abigail's wisdom, Lydia's faithful heart,
Martha's just care, and Mary's better part."

Brief humor was used on the tombstone of Nicholas Eve,
buried in the Parish Burial Ground, Kittery Point, Maine:
"Old and Still"

Even briefer is one that stands in Norris Cemetery,
Damariscotta, Maine:
"Poor Betty."

Frank Fry, of Christian Malford, decided to exhibit his
poetic expertise when he wrote his own epitaph:
> "Here lies I
> Who did die
> I lie did
> As I die did
> Old Frank Fry."

When John Gay died, he was buried in Westminster Abbey
near this interesting thought on stone:
> "Life is a jest, and all things show it:
> I thought so once, but now I know it."

The life of this old gent was quite typical, to say the least:
> "Here lies the body of Sternhold Oakes
> Who lived and died like other folks."

In Rosehill Cemetery, Chicago, Illinois, we find this intriguing comment on the death of Charles DuPlessis:
> "Now Aint
> That Too Bad"

Obviously baffled by what to write, friends of Asenath
Soule prepared the following in Mayflower Cemetery,
Duxbury, Massachusetts:
> "The chisel can't help her any."

Dr. Issac Bartholomew's odd epitaph is found in Hillside
Cemetery, Cheshire, Connecticut:
> "He that was sweet to my repose
> Now is become a stink under my nose."

INDEX